Loving

Life

From A to Z

May God bless you from A to Z !

Norma McMurry

Matthew 6:33

Norma Williams McMurry

ISBN: 978-1-9843-0717-0

Unless otherwise noted, all Scripture quotations are taken from the Holy Bible, New King James Version (NKJV), Copyright © 1982 by Thomas Nelson.

Scriptures noted KJV are from the King James Version, Public Domain

Scriptures noted MSG are from The Message, Copyright © 1993, 2002, 2018 by Eugene H. Peterson

Scriptures noted NIV are from the Holy Bible, New International Version®, NIV® Copyright ©1973, 1978, 1984, 2011 by Biblica, Inc.®

Scriptures noted TLB are from The Living Bible copyright © 1971 by Tyndale House Foundation.

DEDICATION

To Don who encourages me to pursue my passions

To Mother whom I watched read the dictionary for pleasure and entertainment

To Dr. Ellis Joseph who required his tenth-grade English students to memorize the glossary of our literature book and the entirety of **30 Days to a More Powerful Vocabulary**

OTHER BOOKS BY
NORMA MCMURRY
AND
DON MCMURRY

Happily Ever After

Count With Me

Forever Seventeen

CONTENTS

INTRODUCTION

Words fascinate me. I watched my mother read almost daily the seven-inch thick *Webster's New World Dictionary of the American Language Encyclopedic Edition* that occupied a prominent place on a book shelf in our family room. She explained to me that when she was a little girl, her family couldn't afford to buy books, and the two aunts she lived with would not allow her to borrow books from others. She enjoyed reading; they had a dictionary, so she read it for pleasure. My mother acquired an extensive vocabulary.

As an only child, I played games often with my parents. We played Scrabble®, and Mother would use remarkable words. When we traveled in the car, Mother would initiate games in which we named synonyms or antonyms or homophones or homonyms. We even "played" conjugating verbs. At times we identified all the names of people we could think of that started with a certain letter, or named all the flowers or birds we could recall. Looking back, I am amazed at all I learned while playing my mother's games.

I cannot leave out Scripture memorization as part of my informal education. As I learned verse after verse, Mother would emphasize that I needed to know where each verse is found. Knowing the "address" of a passage became important to me. The Bible speaks to all of daily living. Each section of this book reveals Scripture for the subject.

In *Loving Life from A to Z* readers will find entertaining random facts, my opinions, Bible information, practical suggestions, and perhaps ideas you have never thought about before. As I give my thoughts or my favorites on a topic, my desire is that you will think of your favorites for that category, or you will consider your ideas about that matter. Readers will be able to use material from here as enjoyable personal reading, or devotions for family or groups. Several of the sections can be Bible study kick-starters.

Writing this book has been quite fun, but truly stretching as I have researched Scripture and vocabulary for accuracy. I thought I was finished writing several times, but concepts kept coming to mind. I have decided that this is a book that really has no end. Many more subjects could be written. I do not even have my thoughts about church.

I pray that from these pages you will find truths and pleasure from A to Z

A Godly Mother from A to Z

"Behold, children are a heritage from the Lord, The fruit of the womb is a reward." (Psalm 127:3)

Being a mother is such a privilege, but at the same time, it is a lot of work. Frustration comes. Puzzling situations arise, but love abounds. Every day, even in the mundane, a Godly mother will...

Apologize when she is wrong.

Bind physical and emotional wounds.

Consider the differences in the personalities and characteristics of her children.

Discipline each child as the situation requires, and pick her battles carefully.

Encourage her children to be the best that each can be, and to "love the Lord your God with all your heart, with all your soul, with all your mind, and with all your strength." (Mark 12:30)

Follow God's instructions from His Word. "Trust in the Lord with all your heart, And lean not on your own understanding; In all your ways acknowledge Him, And He shall direct your paths." (Proverbs 3:5-6)

Grow in wisdom as her children grow in age.

Help her children develop their abilities and talents.

Ignite the flame given to each child as "the gift of God, which is in you...For God hath not given us the spirit of fear; but of power, and of love, and of a sound mind." (2 Timothy 1:6-7)

Juggle car pools, ball games, recitals, school activities, homework, housework, church, meals, job and myriad responsibilities.

Know she needs help from the Lord, family and others.

Love unconditionally.

Make mistakes, but do her best to correct them and keep going.

Never stop learning and growing as a person and as a mother.

Open her home to her children's friends so she knows they all have a safe place.

Pray daily for her children.

Question what goes on in the community and schools around her children so ungodly influence can be minimized.

Rely on the Holy Spirit for guidance.

Stand strong in her faith in Jesus no matter what circumstances take place. "Yet in all these things we are more than conquerors through Him who loved us." (Romans 8:37)

Try to understand her children's points of view.

Use all her resources to improve her parenting skills.

View her children as gifts from God.

Willfully and faithfully participate in personal and family devotions.

X-out the hurt her children bring into her life, knowing it was not intentional.

Yearn for her children to trust and serve Jesus.

Zip her mouth when the time is appropriate, sensing when to speak and when to stay quiet. "A word fitly spoken is like apples of gold in settings of silver." (Proverbs 25:11)

"Train up a child in the way he should go, And when he is old he will not depart from it." (Proverbs 22:6)

A Good Citizen from A to Z

We know the Bible tell us *"For our citizenship is in heaven, from which we also eagerly wait for the Savior, the Lord Jesus Christ," (Philippians 3:20)*. But until we live in Heaven, we should endeavor to be the best citizen of this world that we can be. God's Word tells us to be loyal to our government until the government tells us to disobey God. *"Let every soul be subject to the governing authorities. For there is no authority except from God, and the authorities that exist are appointed by God." (Romans 13:1-2)*

With these thoughts in mind, a good citizen…

Alerts neighbors to danger.

Builds relationships in the community.

Cares for others in the area.

Dares to speak out.

Energizes others to care about education.

Focuses on what is best for families.

Gives to the poor, charities, and church.

Helps those in need.

Involves him/herself in local affairs.

Juggles responsibilities to be able to give time to others.

Knows his/her neighbors.

Likes to be involved in community projects.

Models wholesome values to others.

Notices needed improvements in infrastructure.

Obeys the laws of the land.

Prays for leaders. (1 Timothy 2:1-4)

Quiets negativism about the community.

Reads the latest updates about issues involving the area.

Studies candidates' views.

Takes seriously the responsibility to support those who protect the nation and the community.

Undertakes to explain community issues to others.

Votes.

Willingly pays proper taxes. (Matthew 22:20-21; Romans 13:6)

eXercises bringing people to justice by serving on juries and supporting law enforcement.

Yields to the laws of the country, state, county, city, and neighborhood.

Zigzags through life's ups and downs to make a better world for family, friends, and community.

A citizen is defined as a native or naturalized person who owes allegiance to a government and is entitled to protection from it

"Therefore submit yourselves to every ordinance of man for the Lord's sake, whether to the king as supreme, or to governors, as to those who are sent by him for the punishment of evildoers and for the praise of those who do good. For this is the will of God, that by doing good you may put to silence the ignorance of foolish men— as free, yet not using liberty as a cloak for vice, but as bondservants of God. Honor all people. Love the brotherhood. Fear God. Honor the king."
(1 Peter 2:13-17)

Actions the Bible Says Take from A to Z

"Then He said to them, 'Follow Me, and I will make you fishers of men.'" (Matthew 4:19)

Abide in Christ. (John 15:4) Settle down; be at home.

Bring your tithes to the Lord's house. (Malachi 3:8-10; Matthew 23:23)

Cast your cares on the Lord. (1 Peter 5:7)

Draw near to God. (James 4:8)

Eat of the Bread of Life. (John 6:57-58)

Flee every form of evil. (1 Thessalonians 5:22)

Go into all the world and preach the gospel to every creature. (Mark 16:15)

Hold your tongue when needful. (James 3:5-12)

Imitate those whose faith led them to be obedient to God. (1 Corinthians 11:1; Hebrews 6:12)

Joy in trials. (James 1:2-3)

Know whom you have believed. (2 Timothy 1:12)

Love your neighbor as yourself. (Luke 10:27; Romans 13:9; Galatians 5:14; James 2:8)

Move mountains with faith. (Matthew 17:19-20)

Name the name of Jesus as Lord. (Acts 4:10; Colossians 3:17; Philippians 2:9-11)

Offer the sacrifice of praise. (Jeremiah 17:26; Jeremiah 33:10-11; Hebrews 13:15)

Persist in prayer. (1 Thessalonians 5:16-18; 2 Timothy 1:3)

Quench the fiery darts of the wicked one. (Ephesians 6:16)

Rejoice in the Lord always. (Philippians 4:4; 1 Thessalonians 5:16)

Separate yourself from the evil of this world. (2 Corinthians 6:16-18)

Teach all nations salvation through Jesus Christ. (Matthew 28:19-20)

Unite with other believers in obedience to Christ. (Psalm 133:1)

Value human life. (Psalm 139:14; 1 John 3:16; John 15:13; Philippians 4:3)

Walk worthy of your calling in Christ. (Colossians 1:10; Ephesians 4:1)

X-ray, or discern, circumstances surrounding you and the world. (Proverbs 18:15)

Yield not to temptation (1 Corinthians 10:13; Matthew 26:41; James 1:12)

Zone your eyes to see others as God sees them. (Luke 10:30-35)

"If anyone desires to come after Me, let him deny himself, and take up his cross daily, and follow Me." (Luke 9:23)

Acts of Kindness from A to Z

"And be kind to one another, tenderhearted,..." (Ephesians 5:32)

Life gets so busy! We can do the urgent and run out of time for what we think are "extra things." Let's try some actions that others find unexpected and unselfish.

Ask about a person's family, especially if they have grandchildren.

Buy someone's lunch, even specify if you like, for military, emergency personnel, a large family with lots of children.

Change a light bulb.

Donate to a worthy cause, or **D**rive someone to an appointment.

Eat with someone who might be lonely.

Fix a meal or someone's brakes.

Go with someone on an errand, or **G**ive a homemade gift.

Help with any chore needed.

Invest in a life, with money, time, kind words, candy, gum, pencil, paper, a book.

Journey to the bed of a sick person.

Keep the charge of a caregiver for a respite from a sick child, or elderly parent.

Lend a hand, or **L**et someone with a few groceries go ahead of you at the checkout counter.

Mow a lawn.

Note someone's accomplishment.

Open a door.

Pay it forward, or **P**ick up trash.

Quiet a crying child by offering to take him/her out of the room where it is important that the parent stay.

Rake leaves.

Smile, **S**peak or **S**end notes.

Take a shopping cart that was left in the lot into the store.

Untie a child's knotted shoelace.

Voice a word of encouragement.

Work with someone who could use a hand.

X-out a debt.

Yield your right-of-way to a driver.

Zip your mouth at the right time.

"And just as you want men to do to you, you also do to them likewise."
(Luke 6:31)

Are There Really Sports from A to Z?

The dictionary defines the noun "sport" as recreation or an activity engaged in such as an athletic event. Hundreds of sports are named in an available list. This is my list; I hope I don't miss your favorite sport.

Archery, Arm Wrestling
Basketball, Baseball, Boxing, Badminton
Curling, Cross Country, Croquet, Chess
Diving, Disc Golf
Equestrian Competitions
Football, Fencing
Gymnastics, Golf
Handball, Hockey
Ice Skating
Jiu-Jitsu
Kneeboarding, Karate
Lacrosse
Motorsports
Nine Pin Bowling
Obstacle Course Racing
Pool, more properly Billiards, Ping Pong
Quidditch
Rugby, Racketball
Soccer, Softball, Swimming

Track and Field, Tennis, Tee-Ball
Unicycling
Volleyball
Wrestling, Water Sports
Xare
Yak Polo
Zorb Football

"And also if anyone competes in athletics, he is not crowned unless he competes according to the rules." (2 Timothy 2:5)

Be Adventurous from A to Z

"And whatever you do, do it heartily, as to the Lord and not to men,"
(Colossians 2:23)

Sometimes you need to do something out of your ordinary routine. You want to bring some extra excitement into your life. Put some activities on your "bucket list," then mark them off as you accomplish them.

Attend the Iditarod Trail Sled Dog Race or the Daytona 500.
Bike a mountain trail.
Crossword puzzles may be new for you.
Drive across America.
Eat international food.
Find antiques for your home.
Genealogy research could bring you surprises.
Host a party for your neighbors.
Initiate an online meal delivery for a sick friend through Meal Train.
Jigsaw puzzles can be frustrating but give great satisfaction when completed.
Kite making and/or flying shows creativity and skill.
Learn a new language.
Make a new friend.
Nab a ticket to a concert, play or, sporting event you want to see.
Open a new savings account.
Play a new sport.

Quit a bad habit.

Read the Bible through and some wonderfully adventurous books.

Sky dive.

Travel.

Undertake a new hobby.

Venture into more education by taking a class.

Watch whales.

Xerox old pictures or old diaries or journals for your children.

Yodel your way into a contest.

Zipline fun is available in many places.

"You will make known to me the path of life; In Your presence is fullness of joy; In Your right hand there are pleasures forever." (Psalm 16:11)

Beautiful Flowers from A to Z

"Consider the lilies, how they grow: they neither toil nor spin; and yet I say to you, even Solomon in all his glory was not arrayed like one of these." (Luke 12:27)

Amaryllis grows a long thick leafless stem which looks stately and impressive. The flowers look like colorful trumpets. My amaryllis came from Sammy, a friend who grew them from his grandmother's. The first time I ever heard the word "amaryllis" was from the lisp of Winthrop in *The Music Man.*

Brown-eyed Susans grew in a huge clump outside my grandmother's dining room and kitchen windows. Daddy would walk with me by them and sing, "Beautiful, beautiful brown-eyes, beautiful, beautiful brown eyes, beautiful, beautiful brown eyes, I'll never love blue-eyes again." He'd squeeze my hand and we'd smile. (I have brown eyes.)

Camellias bloom in myriad colors, shapes, and sizes. It is the state flower of Alabama. The ones outside Grandmother's screened-in porch when I was growing up were so deep pink, they looked almost red. The ones beside my deck now were given to be by Deborah. One bush has pink blooms and one has white.

Daisies grow wild or can be cultivated. My wedding attendants carried white daisies with yellow centers. That was popular in the sixties.

Edelweiss looks so delicate but derives its name from a word meaning noble. I think of the song "Edelweiss" sung by the Von Trapp family as they pledged allegiance to their homeland.

Forsythia blooms in early spring, sending its yellow shoots to brighten the world from winter. When I needed punishment, Mother sent me to the forsythia bush to break a stem. My mind's eye can see her stripping the blossoms from the stalk. I danced as she peppered my legs with that thin twig.

Gardenias give a strong fragrance and lovely white flowers right outside the side door of our house. Don bends to relish an individual blossom every time we walk out that door. Gardenias grew along the side of the Robersonville Primitive Baptist Church. We elementary school children across the street could see and smell them during recess.

Honeysuckle grows wild in our present yard and gives its pungent odor. When I was growing up, we would pick one blossom, pinch the end closest to the stem, pull the stamen and drink that drop of sweet nectar that falls from the flower. Delicious!

Iris bloom in various colors. They need separating after a few years, so I have been given gifts of deep purple, lavender, yellow, burgundy and yellow combination, and white ones from gardener friends.

Jasmine is cultivated for its strong fragrance. It can stand erect or as a vine with white or yellow blossoms. The one I have is a vine with white blossoms. I took it from around our son Joseph's mailbox when they needed to remove it.

Kerria can be known as Japanese Rose or Easter Rose, the latter because of its early spring blooming. It can bloom again later in the summer. Its yellow blooms look like pompons.

Lilac bushes can grow quite large. Their sweet-smelling blooms range in color from lilac to mauve, though some are white. When I was a sophomore in high school, someone brought Mr. Joseph, our English teacher, a vase of lilacs which he placed on a filing cabinet near my desk. They smelled so sweet I became sick and he took them out of the room.

Mums, Football Mums or Homecoming Mums back in the sixties were live, white, four to-five-inch-in-diameter mums made into a corsage that a fellow gave to his date for Homecoming. Ribbons of school colors hung softly from the flower while in the middle, school or fraternity initials were formed with pipe cleaners in one spirit color. Today these mums are made artificially and elaborately, creating a huge industry and one of the largest fundraisers for booster clubs.

Narcissus names the genus of a variety of flowers we commonly call daffodils, buttercups, narcissus, and jonquils. Several dozen species of these cup-shaped flowers flourish. I see them as an announcement that spring will soon be here.

Orchids, in my mind, are associated with Hawaii and corsages. When Jimmy picked me up for our senior prom, he handed me a lovely wrist corsage. I said, "Thank you, this is pretty." He answered, "It ought to be. It cost me three dollars and a half." For many years, I reminded him of that, and we would laugh together.

Pansies lift their pretty faces and bright colors to look like they are happy little flowers. I like that they have such a long blooming season and bloom so late in the year.

Quince can be grown for its fruit or its blooms. The Japanese quince my mother grew looked lovely with its little clusters of deep pink blossoms. But oh, the sharp thorns on those plants! Not fun when retrieving a ball hit or thrown awry!

Roses opened large and bright pink in the southwest corner outside our kitchen window of the home where I grew up. Their vivid yellow stamen stood in sharp contrast to the pink petals. Because of its sheltered location, the bush bloomed most of the year. Tradition called for each person at church on Mother's Day to wear a rose—red if your mother was living, white if she had died. My mother each year I can remember would cut and pin on my dress a pink rose, saying "You wear this, I'm half dead." Then she would laugh. I was the only one at church wearing a pink rose.

Sedum entered my life when a sweet lady in Immanuel Baptist Church, Wilmington, Ohio, gave me plants from her manicured yard. I planted them beside our house in Ohio. They thrived and had pink domed flowers. I moved some to Georgia with us where they flourish. These succulents succeed easily.

Tulips emerge in early spring from underground bulbs. They display showy blooms in various colors. After the flowers fade and the leaves wither in the summer, the plant goes dormant, needs cool temperatures, then shoots through the soil next spring.

Umbrella plant is the name of a houseplant that grows up to six feet tall. The leaves form eight spokes on a stem to look like an umbrella. Because there are eight spokes, the plant is sometimes called an octopus plant.

Violets spread everywhere and have dainty, violet-colored flowers. When I was a little girl, my mother owned a tiny, white, china toothpick holder that she used as a vase when I picked and brought her a handful of violets from our yard.

Wisteria grew up and over the L-shaped front porch of Aunt Annie and Aunt Alice's pre-Civil War home in Conetoe, North Carolina. Its lovely purple blossoms filled the vines and its strong fragrance filled the air. Mother found a small plant under the large vine to bring to Robersonville. She planted it beside our oil drum in the back yard, and let it grow to cover the unsightly drum. Today some friends in Georgia, Nell and Christa, gave me wisteria to climb our fence.

Xeric plants like succulents and cacti make great gardens for areas that tend to have droughts. Many of them have lovely flowers and are easy to maintain.

Yarrow is known as a miracle plant. It quickly stops bleeding, is an anti-inflammatory, an antiseptic, and has enough health benefits to be sold in health food stores. Used in the garden, yarrow enriches the soil. My only experience with yarrow is seeing its blooms scattered wildly like yellow dots in the woods.

Zinnias planted in the vegetable garden not only show off their various bright colors and domed blossoms, they keep out some types of flies while attracting butterflies and hummingbirds. Grandmother always planted a row of zinnias to "help" the garden.

"The grass withers, the flower fades, But the word of our God stands forever." (Isaiah 40:8)

Birds and Why They Are Meaningful to Me from A to Z

"Look at the birds of the air, for they neither sow nor reap nor gather into barns; yet your heavenly Father feeds them. Are you not of more value than they?" (Matthew 6:26)

More than thirty kinds of birds have eaten at our feeders in the last few years. We greatly enjoy watching them land, indulge, selfishly push others away, and display distinct personalities of their kinds. The male cardinal feeds his female at times. The shy towhees scurry under the azalea bush. My mother watched birds from our kitchen window and taught me the names of many.

Albatross—I learned about this bird in ninth-grade literature when we read "The Rime of the Ancient Mariner" by Samuel Taylor Coleridge. I chose to think the bird was good and should not have been shot.

Bluebird—A family of these beautiful birds has nested and cared for little ones in a birdhouse in our back yard for several years straight now. They are so sweet to watch when the fledglings sputter around the grass.

Chickadee and **C**ardinal—In second grade I watched chickadees from our kitchen window and wrote a paper, which I still have, on this tiny, cute bird. The cardinal is the state bird for seven states, the most for any species. I have lived in three of those states.

Dove—From two to eighteen descend together on the ground by the backyard feeder about 10:30 a.m. every day and again about 6:30 p.m. Their low cooing is soothing and peaceful.

Eagle—Congress adopted the Great Seal of the United States in 1782, using the bald eagle with stars and stripes. Through the years the eagle, which from ancient times has been a symbol of strength, appeared on more official American documents, flags and money.

Finch—The most common ones I see are House Finches. The male has a bright red head and lighter red feathers with gray streaks. The female is hard to distinguish from a sparrow. They add color to the group at the feeder and sing beautifully.

Gold Finch—These beauties are bright yellow in the summer and olive in the winter. Of course, the female is duller than the male. This sweet bird is generally monogamous.

Heron—I enjoy seeing a heron or an egret, which I cannot tell apart, standing as still as a statue in shallow water, probably stalking prey. Their long legs and long bills give them an elegant look.

Indigo bunting—This deep-blue bird sings all day long throughout the summer in fields and along roadsides in the Eastern United States. Females are dull brown and mainly stay hidden, caring alone for the eggs and the young after they hatch.

Junco—I sometimes mistake these gray, small birds for chickadees. Juncos usually come to the feeders in flocks, eat seeds from the ground, and make a ticking noise as they fly up to rest in our azalea bush.

Killdeer—For several late springs in a row Don and I visited Laura Baptist Church, and parked beside a "nest" of killdeer eggs. Killdeer like parking lots, rooftops or just a depression in the ground to lay eggs. They protect their nests by scooting around the area on their extremely long, thin legs compared to the size of their bodies, while calling loudly "kill-dee-dee" and "kill-deer" over and over. Their eggs looked just like the rocks in the parking lot. Consequently, they have become one of my favorite birds.

Lark—Social birds, the horned larks can be found in large flocks and with other birds like snow buntings and longspurs. They creep along bare ground searching for small seeds and insects. The horned lark is the only lark found in North America. The male has a black mask and tiny black hornlike feathers that stick straight up on either side of his head.

Mockingbird—I grew up listening to the mockingbirds copy the songs of every bird around. They were constantly happy sounding and never quit singing. One of my favorite songs on the television show Your Hit Parade in 1951 sung by Dorothy Collins was "Mockingbird Hill."

Tra-la-la twiddly-dee-dee-dee it gives me a thrill
To wake up in the morning to the mockingbird's trill...

Nuthatch—Two kinds, the white breasted with their blue-grey backs and the brown headed, visit our backyard feeder every day. It is fun to watch them walk head first down the nearby tree. Looking for insects, they use their strong beaks and show their large heads and short tails.

Owl—Our grandsons in Charlotte, North Carolina, show me the limbs where two owls sit in their back yard. One afternoon when we heard the owl hooting, we rushed to the tree to find him sitting proudly in his spot, talking to anyone who would listen.

Partridge—The famous one is "in a pear tree." These birds are not native to America, but are brought over and raised in captivity to be used as game birds in hunting.

Quail—Mother called these birds Bobwhites. Periodically we saw a proud mother walking close to a wooded area along the edge of the road with her brood of four or five chicks marching in a line behind her. Their slow, distinct and deliberate call of "bob-WHITE" still thrills me. We saw them in the wild, but quail are also farmed for meat and for eggs.

Robin—Whenever I see the first robin of the year, I know he is a sign that Spring is on its way. When I taught at Sinclair Community College in Dayton, Ohio, I could look out my classroom window in late February or early March and see as many as thirty robins pecking at the ground. I enjoyed that sight.

Sparrow—They seem to be the most numerous little birds of them all. They certainly acclimate to having people around. When we eat outside at a restaurant, sparrows often hop close by to grab crumbs. Our cat Dream sits directly under our bird feeder and the sparrows do not mind.

Tufted titmouse and Towhee—Little crested gray tufted titmice frequent our feeders daily. They assert themselves, making other birds move over or leave. Their acrobatics entertain us. Towhee is a fairly new bird to me. They are extremely shy birds who stay in the bushes, even nest low in bushes or on the ground, and move quickly across the grass to eat on the ground under the feeder.

Upland sandpiper—On visits to the ocean, I watch these wader shorebirds run quickly to dig their long bills into the sand for small invertebrates as waves recede. Their long, thin legs move fast and I smile.

Vultures—Oh, they look repulsive eating carrion from the road, but I have fond memories of looking for turkey buzzards making circles above the trees and talking with Daddy about what could be dead below them.

Wren and Woodpecker—We call our wren Wrenny. He and his mate grace our deck, eat at the feeder, and sit on the fence daily. They sing loudly and build nests in several places. Two of their three eggs hatched in a flower pot on our deck a few weeks ago. I kept Dream from the deck the day the fledglings hopped around under the strict watch of Wrenny and their mother. Beautiful describes our amazing woodpeckers. Those who visit us include, downy, hairy, ladder backed, red-bellied, and red-headed. They all want suet for dinner.

Xantus's hummingbird—Actually this beautiful species is found only in California, but it started with an X. The hummingbirds who visit us are ruby-throated. Their wings move so fast they look almost invisible. The tiny creatures enjoy our butterfly bush and other flowers as well as their red feeder.

Yellow-eyed penguin—Or any penguin! I have seen penguins only in zoos or water shows. Living roughly half their lives in water and half on land, they eat fish or other sea life that they catch while they are swimming. My favorite aspect of these flightless birds is their tuxedo-like look and their waddling walk. The fact that they mate for life and both parents care for the egg/s and then the young, endears penguins to me.

Zirds of all kinds—My mother and daddy subscribed to the Raleigh News and Observer. One morning the caption under a picture of birds misprinted the word "birds" as "zirds." Our family joke for the rest of my growing up became "look at the zirds."

"I know all the birds of the mountains, and the wild beasts
of the field are Mine." (Psalm 50:11)

Christmas Thoughts from A to Z

"For unto us a Child is born, ..." (Isaiah 9:6).

Christmas, just the word, evokes many thoughts and emotions for each of us. First we think of the birth of our Savior, closely followed by sights, sounds, smells, symbols, scurrying, shopping, sending, and such. Loving and giving, family and friends, come to mind. So let's look at Christmas from A to Z.

Angel was privileged to announce Christ's birth to the shepherds. (Luke 2:8-12)

Birth gave Christ human form. (Galatians 4:4) **B**ells around the world toll annaully as we celebrate.

Christ, the Son of God and Son of Man, is the central figure of Christmas.

Donkey is never mentioned in the Scripture of the Christmas story, yet I think of a donkey as a Christmas figure. The Bible says Joseph and Mary went from Nazareth to Bethlehem (Luke 2:4-5). The mode of transportation in that day was a donkey. Plus, we always have a donkey in the nativity scene.

Evergreen is a symbol of immortality and eternity. We use trees and branches as decorations.

Family loves to get together at Christmas. They exchange gifts, sing, laugh, eat, and celebrate the birth of their Savior.

Garlands form adornments for majesty, honor, and beauty.

Holly is also known as Holy Tree or Christ's Thorn. The leaves are symbolic of the thorns Christ wore when He was crucified, and the tiny red berries represent the blood Christ shed.

I personally appreciate that the world sets aside a day we call Christmas to acknowledge the birth of our Savior and His changing of the world.

Jesus was born! (Luke 2:11) There is no Christmas without Jesus.

King Herod ruled in Jerusalem when Jesus was born and became concerned when the wise men told him they were searching for the new King. When the wise men did not return to Herod, he ordered every male child two years old and under to be killed. Joseph, warned by an angel, took Mary and Jesus to Egypt. (Matthew 2:1-17)

Lights decorate our Christmas trees, yards, houses, and stores at Christmas. It is appropriate that our Christmas celebration be filled with light as we celebrate Jesus, the "Light of the world." (John 8:12)

Manger is the place Mary laid Jesus, showing His humble birth. (Luke 2:7)

Nativity, when capitalized, indicates the birth of Jesus. Many families collect Nativity sets. Is your favorite made of paper by a child, china from a store, or olive wood from the Holy Land? Don carved us a Nativity set of basswood which I keep displayed on our dining room table all year.

Ornaments are used to decorate and remind us of happy times. Some are made by children or others who give them to us.

Presents represent tangible expressions of love for the receivers. The wise men presented gifts to Jesus when they encountered Him. (Matthew 2:11)

Quest of the wise men from the East led to worship of the King. (Matthew 2:1-12)

Reading the Christmas story from Luke 2 and Matthew 2 is a tradition for many families.

Shepherds did their nightly job when they were surprised by the angel with the special announcement. (Luke 2:8-12)

Testimony has to be a vital Christmas word. During Christmastime, we have opportunities to tell what Christ means in our lives to those who may be more receptive at Christmas.

Unite our hearts in Christ is a prayer we offer to God at Christmas. As we give to missions and to those who need items or cheer, we need to work together in Christ's name.

Visiting family and friends brightens Christmas for everyone.

Wreaths have had many meanings through the centuries, especially concerning welcoming and giving. The Christmas wreath adds a spiritual meaning of eternal life symbolized by the circle and the evergreen.

Xylophone is an example of a toy that delights children when received at Christmas, and delights givers when children show their excitement.

Yuletide greetings given and received say I love you and Merry Christmas.

Zenith of holidays describes Christmas in the hearts of many.

"...unto us a Son is given; and the government will be upon His shoulder. And His name will be called Wonderful, Counselor, Mighty God, Everlasting Father, Prince of Peace. Of the increase of His government and peace there will be no end," (Isaiah 9:6-7)

"Eternal" Explained from A to Z

"He has made everything beautiful in its time. Also He has put eternity in their hearts, except that no one can find out the work that God does from beginning to end." (Ecclesiastes 3:11)

When I was a teenager, a popular song included the words, "...until the twelfth of never, and that's a long, long time." At our slumber parties, we girls knew that was how long we would "go steady" with our present boyfriends. At the next slumber party, the boyfriends more than likely had changed. God's love for us is eternal and never fails. The life He gives us never ends. "Eternal" can be described as:

Always
Beyond beyond
Counting to the last number
Dot, dot, dot
Everlasting
Forever
Greater than greater than >
Higher than high
Infinity ∞
Just a little more
Keeping on keeping on
Longer than long
More and more
Never-ending

Only a little further
Perpetual
Quadrillions then more
Redemption
Salvation
Till
Unending
Value of Jesus' sacrifice
Walking in a circle till it ends
eXtending further
Your debt to God's grace and mercy
Zillions plus

"For thus says the High and Lofty One Who inhabits eternity,
whose name is Holy: 'I dwell in the high and holy place,
With him who has a contrite and humble spirit,
To revive the spirit of the humble,
And to revive the heart of the contrite ones.'"
(Isaiah 57:15)

Everyone Needs from A to Z

"For your heavenly Father knows that you need all these things."
(Matthew 6:32)

Everyone needs:

Affirmation
Belonging
Compassion
Discipline
Energy
Faith
Gifts
Help
Interests
Justification
Kindness
Love
Manners
Nourishment
Opinions
Prayer
Quiet times
Rest
Sunshine

Touches
Understanding
Value
Water
eXcitement
Yearnings
Zeal

"You aren't alive if you aren't in need."
Henry Cloud, **Safe People: How to Find Relationships That Are Good for You and Avoid Those That Aren't***, first published 1995 by Zondervon.*

From My Deck from A to Z

"Then God saw everything that He had made, and indeed it was very good." (Genesis 1:31)

On our deck, admiring God's beautiful world from where I sit, I see, hear, or smell the following:

Air, cool and refreshing, and **A**zaleas teeming with color.

Birds devouring seeds from our feeders, their **B**abies nearby hopping, fluttering, and crying for food; **B**eans in Don's garden, growing up his staked **B**amboo poles; and **B**ees buzzing on **B**looms.

Clouds in the sky, taking shapes of objects I could name, then dissipating to wisps of fluff; **C**hipmunks gathering seeds from under the bird feeders till their little cheeks look like they will burst, then scampering under the deck to their dens somewhere to store their goods.

Dirt that Don has dumped atop the plot of red clay to help his garden grow.

Evergreens standing stately, seeming to know that other trees get a winter look while they keep their color.

Fence separating our back yard from the rest of the world and making private the little area in my view; **F**rogs, probably toads, digging their shallow little cave-houses in the pine straw.

Grass growing too quickly and **G**arden growing slowly; **G**ardenias wafting their wonderful smell over their domain.

Hornets humming while flying too close to me for comfort; **H**umming birds actually perching on a branch of a crepe myrtle. I didn't realize they stopped to rest.

Iris standing tall, reminding me of friends who generously gave them to us.

June bugs, flying up from the grass, landing on a table nearby and tucking their wings in so close to their bodies that the bugs look like they have shells on their backs.

Knotweed poking its head up in the grass as if to say, "You can't get rid of me."

Leaves rustling in the breeze, moving in the wind; Lizards listlessly lying in the sun.

Morning glories, reminding me of days long ago when my joyful daddy would sing, "Nothing could be finer than to be in Carolina in the morning. No one could be sweeter than my sweetie when I meet her in the morning. Where the morning glories twine around my door, whispering pretty stories I long to hear once more..." He smiled BIG when he sang and he sang often.

Nests, decorating the deck, with the wasps controlling the light fixture and the wrens thinking every flower pot is a place for their twigs and leaves.

Orange black-eyed Susans, looking bright, reminding me to pray for Iva, the sweet friend who lovingly dug them and gave them to me.

Pine trees, lots of them, bending with the breezes high above the rest of our backyard action, and letting go of their needles and cones which fall gracefully to the ground.

Queues of zinnias, adding vivid colors to the yard, but wanting to be cut so more blooms will come.

Rays of sunshine streaming through the trees, looking almost like I could walk up them right into heaven.

Squirrels entertaining me with their playful antics, chasing each other around trees, over the fence, and then resting on the bird bath; Spiders weaving webs constantly. Sparrows darting around from the feeders to the bushes to the trees and back to the feeders.

Trees growing in every stage—tiny seedlings to large trunks, blooming mimosa to waxy magnolia leaves.

Utter glory of God the Creator, shining brightly through His creation.

Vines stretching their fingers further and further from the root, creeping over whatever they find in their way.

Water, providing refreshment for the animals and the plants, and giving bathing opportunities to the birds; Weeds, rising relentlessly as if to say, "You may not want us here, but we're not leaving."

Xeroxed description of quietness and beauty, renewing my body and soul.

Yard for games and fun with family and friends, especially our grandchildren.

Zoology classes could benefit from a field trip to our back yard to study these animals, their habits, and their antics.

"This is my Father's world, and to my list'ning ears,
all nature sings, and round me rings the music of the spheres.
This is my Father's world, I rest me in the thought of rocks and trees,
of skies and seas; His hands the wonders wrought."
This Is My Father's World by Maltbie D. Babcock

Giving Thanks for Life from A to Z

"Be thankful to Him, and bless His name. For the LORD is good;"
(Psalm 100:4)

Different seasons in our lives give us different aspects for which to be thankful. This list is from my perspective as an older person. I am extremely thankful for:

Ability to keep active and go to events for family and church.

Biblical principles that I have learned always work. God never changes. (Hebrews 13:8)

Children—they are truly a gift from God. How I love their laughter and energy. (Psalm 127:3)

Doctors who treat with concern our physical bodies.

Energy to walk and exercise for health, and do needed chores.

Friends both old and new.

Godly people to look to for examples and advice.

Happiness of those around me.

Internet to connect with family, old friends and new friends.

Jello that my grandchildren delight in my making.

Kisses from my grandkids and granddogs.

Lovely pictures our children send of their families and pictures of graduates and brides sent from friends.

Memories of school days, young adult days, and many relationships in my life.

Nights of fellowship with neighbors, church friends, and family.

Owning one beautiful Persian cat, Dream, who provides hours of pleasure.

Pastors who preach the Word and love their flocks.

Quiet times when I remember the past, enjoy the present, and look forward to the future.

Restaurants that give senior discounts.

Stars to watch and make wishes on.

Teachers of all kinds, from my early life till today when I am still learning.

Understanding friends and family when I get about slower than I used to.

Vacations with our children and their families.

Wedding the man I did over 54 years ago.

Xmas. Some people don't like Christmas written this way. The first letter of the word Christ in the Greek alphabet is X (Chi) so writing Christmas with the Greek letter is honoring Christ.

Yellow game pieces. When others ask for red, green, and blue, I enjoy the yellow because I am so glad they are playing board games.

Zoos because they are places where I can see animals I would never otherwise see.

"And whatever you do in word or deed, do all in the name of the Lord Jesus, giving thanks to God the Father through Him."
(Colossians 3:17)

God Gave Us Fruit from A to Z

*"Then God said, 'Let the earth bring forth grass, the herb that yields seed, and the **fruit** tree that yields **fruit** according to its kind, whose seed is in itself, on the earth;' and it was so."*
(Genesis 1:11)

Besides being delicious, fruit is generally known for its nutritional value. Fruit contains vitamins and minerals that promote good health. Jaclyn London, the director of Good Housekeeping Institute, says in her research, "When it comes to eating more produce, you can't go wrong. Every fruit is a great option. Eating fruit boosts mood and reduces the risk of heart disease, obesity, and type 2 diabetes. The fiber in fruit also supports better digestion."

When Don and I had the privilege of going to St. Lucia on a mission trip, we saw extraordinary kinds of fruit beautifully hanging on trees. God created for us fruit from A to Z.

Apple
Banana
Cherry
Dewberry
Elderberry
Fig
Grapefruit
Honeydew
Ita Palm
Java Plum

Kiwi

Lemon

Mango

Noni

Orange

Peach

Quince

Raspberries

Strawberry

Tangerine

Ugli

Victoria Plum

Watermelon

Xylocarp, such as coconut

Yali Pear

Zinfandel Grape

"And we made ordinances to bring the firstfruits of our ground and the firstfruits of all fruit of all trees, year by year, to the house of the Lord;"
(Nehemiah 10:35)

God Is…(adjective) from A to Z

"But whoever keeps His word, truly the love of God is perfected in him. By this we know that we are in Him. (1 John 2:5)

God is:

Able. (Ephesians 3:20)

Benevolent. (James 1:17)

Caring. (1 Peter 5:7)

Dependable. (Zephaniah 3:5)

Everlasting. (Psalm 90:2)

Faithful. (1 Corinthians 1:9)

Gracious. (Psalm 116:5)

Holy. (Psalm 99:9)

Immortal, Invisible. (1 Timothy 1:17)

Just. (Psalm 7:11)

Knowable. (1 John 2:3)

Loving. (John 3:16)

Merciful. (Psalm 116:5)

Nurturing. (Isaiah 66:13 NIV)

Omnipresent. (Psalm 139:7-12)

Powerful. (Jeremiah 32:17)

Quickening. (Romans 8:11 KJV)

Righteous. (Psalm 116:5)

Strong. (Job 9:4)

Tender. (Psalm 69:16)

Unchanging. (Hebrews 13:8)

Victorious. (1 Chronicles 29:11)

Willing that none should perish. (2 Peter 3:9)

e**X**emplary. (1 Peter 2:21 NIV)

Yoke-bearing. (Matthew 11:28)

Zeroth. (Isaiah 43:10; Exodus 3:14)

"For if our heart condemns us, God is greater than our heart,
and knows all things." (1 John 3:20)

God: The Father, Son, and Holy Spirit is…(noun)from A to Z

"…for He is Lord of lords and King of kings; and those who are with Him are called, chosen, and faithful." (Revelation 17:14)

Adoni, Hebrew for "my lord." (Joshua 5:14)

Banner. (Exodus 17:15)

Christ. (John 14:9)

Defense. (Psalm 59:9)

Elohim, a plural Hebrew word, the first name given for God in His word. (Genesis 1:1)

Father. (Matthew 6:9)

Guide. (Psalm 32:8)

Helper. (Psalm 54:4)

Inheritance. (Psalm 16:5-6)

Judge. (Psalm 7:11)

King. (Psalm 47:7)

Love. (1 John 4:8)

Master. (Luke 17:13)

Nail in a sure place. (Isaiah 22:22-24 KJV) Though this Scripture describes Eliakim, it is a Messianic prophecy of Jesus, the One on whom all burdens can be placed.

Omega. (Revelation 1:8)

Peace. (Isaiah 9:6)

Quickener. (1 Timothy 6:13 KJV)

Redeemer. (Job 19:25)

Salvation. (Psalm 62:7)

Truth. (John 14:6)

Unifier. (1 Corinthians 12:12)

Vine. (John 15:5)

Water. (John 4:10)

Xavier. In the Urban Dictionary this is a person who tells people how to become better. He knows what to say in any situation. He is loving, kind, and generous. (Psalm 34:8)

Yahweh. (Exodus 3:13-14) Yahweh is Hebrew for God.

Zenith. The dictionary describes a zenith as the top or apex, when something is powerful or successful. (Psalm 66:7)

"Therefore God also has highly exalted Him and given Him the name which is above every name, that at the name of Jesus every knee should bow, of those in heaven, and of those on earth, and of those under the earth,"
(Philippians 2:9-10)

God Made Dads Special from A to Z

Many fathers in the Bible did not relate well to their children. David was busy fighting for land and his life, leaving his children in the care of others. (1 Chronicles 27:32) The priest Eli did not discipline his sons, letting them become vile. (1 Samuel 3:13) God desires that fathers be active in the bringing up of their children. Living in obedience to God's Word, a dad will:

Acknowledge the Lordship of Christ in his life and home.
(Deuteronomy 4:9; 6:4))
Build his marriage so his children know he loves his wife.
(Ephesians 5:25)
Cherish relationships with family and friends. (John 13:34)
Direct his family in the ways of God. (Proverbs 22:6)
Energize his children to develop their talents and abilities.
(Ephesians 2:10)
Fight for the hearts of his family. (Malachi 4:5-6)
Gather his family to read God's word together. (Deuteronomy 6:4-7)
Hear the still, small voice of God for direction. (1 Kings 19:12)
Instruct his children in the ways of the Lord. (Proverbs 1:8)
Judge the cultural landscape and discuss God's ways with his children.
(Titus 2:11-12)
Kindle the flame in his children's hearts for the gift of God.
(2 Timothy 1:6)
Lead his family daily in devotions. (Psalm 61:8)
Model the values that he is teaching. (Proverbs 8:32)

Need to admit when he is wrong. (1 John 1:9)

Order his steps in the ways of the Lord. (Psalm 37:23)

Pray for and with his children. (1 Samuel 12:23)

Quit bad or unhealthy habits. (1 Corinthians 9:27)

Realize he cannot meet every expectation of those around him.
(2 Corinthians 12:9)

See the importance of spending time with his children.
(Deuteronomy 6:7)

Treat each child with respect and listen to what he or she has to say.
(Proverbs 1:5)

Uniquely view each child in light of his or her personality.
(Proverbs 2:1-5)

Visualize the future for his children so he can work toward goals.
(Psalm 37:4)

Work to provide food and shelter for his family. (2 Thessalonians 3:10)

eXtend grace and mercy along with discipline for his children.
(Proverbs 3:12; Hebrews 12:11)

Yield his life to align with God's truth. (Mark 12:30)

Zealously seek God's best for his family. (3 John 4)

*And you, fathers, do not provoke your children to wrath, but bring them
up in the training and admonition of the lord. (Ephesians 6:4)*

God's Love Is...from A to Z

"For God so loved the world that He gave His only begotten Son, that whoever believes in Him should not perish but have everlasting life."
(John 3:16)

God's love is:

Abiding. (1 John 4:12)

Beautiful blessing. (Deuteronomy 23:5)

Compelling. (2 Corinthians 5:14)

Delightful. (2 Chronicles 9:8)

Everlasting. (Jeremiah 31:3)

Forgiving. (1 John 1:9)

Gracious. (Amos 5:15)

Helpful. (Psalm 54:4)

Infinite. (Ephesians 3:14-19)

Jealous. (Deuteronomy 4:23-24)

Kind. (Joel 2:13)

Limitless. (Jude 1:21)

Merciful. (Ephesians 2:4)

Near. (Hebrews 7:19)

Overt. (Romans 8:31)

Patient. (2 Thessalonians 3:5; Psalm 86:15)

Quieting. (Zephaniah 3:17)

Refreshing. (2 Corinthians 13:14)

Steadfast. (Daniel 6:26)

Total. (2 John 1:3)

Understanding. (Psalm 147:5)

Vital. (Psalm 40:17)

Warning. (Proverbs 3:12)

Xenial. (Zephaniah 3:17)

Yours. (2 Corinthians 13:14)

Zealous. (Joel 2:18-32)

"...that Christ may dwell in your hearts through faith; that you, being rooted and grounded in love, may be able to comprehend with all the saints what is the width and length and depth and height—to know the love of Christ which passes knowledge; that you may be filled with all the fullness of God." (Ephesians 3:17-19)

God's Promises from A to Z

For no matter how many promises God has made,
they are "Yes" in Christ. (2 Corinthians 1:20 NIV)

Abide in Him and He will abide in you. (John 15:4)

Blessings you can't imagine await those who tithe their resources to God. (Malachi 3:10)

Confess your sins and He will forgive and cleanse. (1 John 1:9)

Death, the last enemy, has been conquered. (1Corinthians 15:50-57)

Eyes have not seen all that God has prepared for those who love Him. (1 Corinthians 2:9)

Forever we can be with Him if we believe Christ gave His life for our sins. (John 3:16)

God will supply all your needs. (Philippians 4:19)

He will hear and answer prayer. (John 15:7)

If you ask God for wisdom, He will give it to you. (James 1:5)

Joy comes in the morning. (Psalm 30:5)

Know that God will be exalted among the nations. (Psalm 46:10)

Lean not on your understanding; acknowledge Him, and He will direct you. (Proverbs 3:5-6)

Mercy of God towards us endures forever. (Psalm 136:1)

Nothing can separate us from the love of God. (Romans 8:38-39)

Only Jesus can save your soul. (John 14:6)

Peace is here for you. (John 14:27)

Quietness and confidence will give you His strength. (Isaiah 30:15)

Rest is offered to those who are burdened. (Matthew 11:28)

Strength for each day is available. (Deuteronomy 33:25)

Temptations can be overcome. (1 Corinthians 10:13)

Uttered groanings by the Holy Spirit intercede when we do not know what to pray. (Romans 8:26)

Victory is given by God through Jesus Christ. (1 Corinthians 15:57)

Whoever loses his life for Christ's sake, will save it. (Luke 9:24)

eXceedingly wonderful things are prepared for those who love God. (1 Corinthians 2:9)

You will reap what you sow. (Galatians 6:7)

Zeal of the Lord establishes an everlasting Kingdom. (Isaiah 9:7)

"Standing on the promises of Christ my King, Through eternal ages let His praises ring, Glory in the highest, I will shout and sing, Standing on the promises of God."
Standing on the Promises R.Kelso Carter 1886

Grandchildren Are... from A to Z

"Children's children are the crown of old men, And the glory of children is their father." (Proverbs 17:6)

Grandchildren are:

Adorable.
Blessings.
Certainly life's bonus.
Delightful.
Energetic.
Fun.
Great.
Heartwarming.
Intriguing.
Just about perfect.
Knowledgeable.
Lovely.
Marvelous.
Naughty at times, but truly **N**ice.
Often your biggest fans.
Part of your legacy.
Quite photogenic.
Really special.
Super.

Totally worth any energy or time investment.

Utterly fantastic.

Valuable.

Wonderful.

eXciting.

Your pals in not telling parents everything that happens when you are together.

Zesty.

"Only take heed to yourself, and diligently keep yourself, lest you forget the things your eyes have seen, and lest they depart from your heart all the days of your life. And teach them to your children and your grandchildren," (Deuteronomy 4:9)

Have You Ever Felt From A to Z

"A sound mind makes for a robust body, but runaway emotions corrode the bones. (Proverbs 14:30 MSG)

Emotions can run our lives if we are not careful. We need to live by what we know to be true rather than what we feel. Our feelings can fool us. Have you ever felt:

Affirmed or **A**ngry
Blessed or **B**itter
Courageous or **C**onfused
Delighted or **D**oubtful
Enthusiastic or **E**nvious
Fervent or **F**earful
Grateful or **G**rieved
Happy or **H**urt
Independent or **I**nsignificant
Joyful or **J**ealous
Kind or **K**icked down
Loved or **L**onely
Merry or **M**iserable
Nice or **N**eglected
Optimistic or **O**verwhelmed
Pleasant or **P**ained
Quiet or **Q**ualmed

Relieved or **R**ejected
Secure or **S**orrowful
Trusting or **T**roubled
Uplifted or **U**pset
Victorious or **V**ulnerable
Warm inside or **W**orried
e**X**cited or e**X**cluded
Youthful or **Y**ucky
Zesty or **Z**estless

"A fool vents all his feelings, But a wise man holds them back."(Proverbs 29:11)

Homophones from A to Z

According to Merriam-Webster dictionary homophones are two or more words pronounced alike but different in meaning or derivation or spelling. Homophones in the Bible are Abel and able. Pronounced the same, Abel is a son of Adam and Eve, while able describes having the power or resources to make something happen. There are homophones from A to Z.

*"Then she bore again, this time his brother **Abel**. Now Abel was a keeper of sheep, but Cain was a tiller of the ground." (Genesis 4:2)*

*"And Moses chose **able** men out of all Israel, and made them heads over the people:" (Exodus 18:25)*

Ad (advertisement), Add (combine)

Bread (baked food), Bred (produced)

Chews (gnaw with teeth), Choose (select)

Deer (animal), Dear (highly valued)

Ere (before), Heir (one who inherits)

Facts (true things), Fax (document sent over the phone)

Gait (stride), Gate (opening in a fence)

Here (this place), Hear (aware of with the ear)

Isle (island), Aisle (a passageway separating rows), I'll (contraction for I will)

Jeans (pants), Genes (sequence of DNA on a chromosome)

Know (aware of), No (refuse)

Lead (metal), Led (past tense of lead as to guide)

Meat (edible part of animal), Meet (get together)

Night (sun is down), Knight (rank of merit)

Our (belonging to us), Hour (time of sixty minutes)

Pare (cut), Pair (two), Pear (fruit)

Queue (line), Cue (prompt)

Read (understand written words), Reed (kind of tall grass)

See (aware of with the eyes), Sea (large body of water)

Their (belonging to them), There (a place)

Urn (vase), Earn (work for)

Vain (no worth), Vein (blood vessel), Vane (movable object to show direction)

Wholly (entire), Holy (righteous)

Xi (fourteenth letter of Greek alphabet), Sigh (deep breath that can be heard)

You (second person pronoun), Ewe (female sheep)

Zinc (metal element), Zink (sixteenth century church musical instrument)

*"So Joshua said to the children of Israel, 'Come **here**, and **hear** the words of the Lord your God.'" (Joshua 3:9)*

*"So they loaded **their** donkeys with the grain and departed from **there**." (Genesis 42:26)*

In Christ I Am from A to Z

"Therefore, if anyone is in Christ, he is a new creation; old things have passed away; behold, all things have become new." (2 Corinthians 5:17)

In Christ, I am...

Alive to have an abundant life. (1 Corinthians 15:22; John 10:10)

Blessed with the promise of the Spirit through faith. (Galatians 3:14)

Called to have a child-like faith and trust. (Matthew 18:2-3)

Delivered from the darkness of sin and brought into His kingdom. (Colossians 1:13)

Established in His promises. (2 Corinthians 1:20-22)

Forgiven and instructed to forgive others. (Ephesians 4:32)

Guaranteed a home in Heaven. (John 14:1-3)

Helped in times of trouble and need. (Psalm 46:1)

Invited to dine with Him, at His table in His kingdom. (Luke 22:29-30)

Justified freely by His grace. (Romans 3:24)

Kept by the power of God until He takes me to Heaven. (2 Timothy 1:12; 1 Peter 1:5)

Lifted by His love and grace from a life of sin to a life with Him. (Psalm 3:2-4)

Made a new creation. (2 Corinthians 5:17)

Never alone. (Hebrews 13:5)

Open to listen to the promptings of His Spirit. (John 16:13)

Partaking in the promises of God through the gospel. (Ephesians 3:6)

Quieted and comforted in all of life. (Psalm 23)

Reconciled to God. (2 Corinthians 5:19)

Steadfast in my faith in Him. (Colossians 2:5; 1 Corinthians 15:58)

Triumphant in all of life's circumstances. (2 Corinthians 2:14)

Unconditionally loved. (Ephesians 3:14-19)

Victorious over death and the grave. (1 Corinthians 15:54-57)

Walking in the truth. (John 8:32; 3 John 4)

e**X**tremely grateful for the guidance He gives for living. (John 16:13; Isaiah 58:11)

Yearning to tell others of His grace, mercy, and love for them. (Matthew 28:19-20)

Zealous to repent of my wrongs and live to please Him. (Revelation 3:19-20)

"for in Him we live and move and have our being,..." Acts 17:28a

Love Is NOT...from A to Z

"And though I bestow all my goods to feed the poor, and though I give my body to be burned, but have not love, it profits me nothing."(1 Corinthians 13:3)

Love is NOT:

Arrogant.

Boastful.

Conceited.

Devious.

Envious.

Fickle.

Greedy.

Haughty.

Irritable.

Jealous.

Kept.

Lustful.

Manipulative.

Narcissistic.

Oppressive.

Proud.

Quick to judge.

Resentful.

Selfish.
Temperamental.
Unkind.
Vicious.
Wanton.
Xenophobic.
Yelling.
Zany.

"He who does not love does not know God, for God is love."
(1 John 4:8)

Memorable Moments of Men in the Bible
from A to Z

"God, who at various times and in various ways spoke in time past to the
fathers by the prophets, has in these last days spoken to us
by His *Son,..." (Hebrews 1:1)*

Abraham left his home in obedience to God and traveled when he did not know where God was leading him. (Genesis 12:1-2)

Benjamin was Joseph's younger brother of their mother Rachel who died in childbirth. (Genesis 35:16-18)

Christ humbled Himself to take the form of a man born of a virgin, endured the cross and is seated at the right hand of the Father. (Philippians 2:5-11; Hebrews 12:2)

David sinned greatly, asked for forgiveness, and was described by God as "a man after My own heart, who will do all My will." (Acts 13:22)

Daniel prayed faithfully, against the king's decree, to the living God, then God sent an angel to shut the mouth of lions when the rulers threw Daniel into the lions den. (Daniel 6)

Elijah faced the prophets of Baal on Mt. Carmel with God bringing victory by sending fire to accept the sacrifice Elijah offered, then sending rain after a time of drought. (1 Kings 18).

Felix, the unscrupulous Roman governor of Judea, listened to Paul's witness concerning Jesus Christ, but as men and women do today, answered, "Go away for now; when I have a convenient time I will call for you." (Acts 24)

Gideon judged Israel while they were under the Midianites, and God gave them victory using three hundred valiant men, torches, and pitchers. (Judges 7)

Hezekiah, King of Judah, trusted God for victory when others told him defeat was imminent. When he was sick, Hezekiah's prayer moved God to give him fifteen more years. As a sign of God's healing, God moved the shadow of the sun dial back ten degrees. (2 Kings 19-20)

Isaiah prophesied to Judah during the reign of four kings. When he "...heard the voice of the Lord, saying: 'Whom shall I send, and who will go for Us?' Then (he) said, 'Here am I! Send me.'" (Isaiah 6:8) Christians today need to answer God's call with the reply Isaiah gave.

Joshua succeeded Moses to lead the children of Israel into the Promised Land. God told Joshua He would be with him as He was with Moses. God's words mean much to us today. "Have I not commanded you? Be strong and of good courage; do not be afraid, nor be dismayed, for the Lord your God is with you wherever you go." (Joshua 1:9)

Korah, a Levite, along with Dathan and Abiram, led 250 disgruntled Israelites to rebel against Moses and Aaron. While those men stood in front of their tents, God opened the ground to swallow them and all their families. He also sent fire to consume the 250 who followed the rebellion. Do not go against the leaders God appoints! (Numbers 16)

Lazarus died and was buried four days when Jesus raised him from the dead. (John 11)

Moses led the children of Israel out of the bondage of Egypt and instituted the Passover. (Exodus 12-13)

Noah built an ark per God's instructions to save his family when God destroyed the whole earth with a flood. (Genesis 6:13-22)

Onesimus left his master Philemon as a lost man, but while encountering Paul became a Christian. Paul appealed to Philemon to take Onesimus back as a brother. (Philemon)

Peter denied three times that he knew Christ. After the look that lasted a lifetime (Luke 22:61), Peter became loyal to the Lord until his death. (John 21:15-19)

Quirinius governed Syria during the time the census was taken when Jesus was born in Bethlehem. (Luke 2:2)

Rehoboam became king when his father Solomon died. Because he did not follow the advice of the elders of Israel, Jeroboam took all the kingdom except those dwelling in the cities of Judah. When Rehoboam gathered the men of Judah and Benjamin to fight to restore his kingdom, the prophet Shemaiah told him not to go to war. Rehoboam obeyed. (1Kings 11:43-12:24)

Simeon, led by the Holy Spirit, went to the temple to hold the Child Jesus in his arms and declare Him to be, "A light to bring revelation to the Gentiles, and the glory of Your people Israel."(Luke 2:25-35)

Timothy, whom Paul referred to as "my beloved and faithful son in the Lord," (1 Corinthians 4:17) traveled with and for Paul and served with him in the gospel ministry. (Philippians 2:22)

Uriah, one of David's mighty men and husband of Bathsheba, served faithfully in David's army. Because David called for Bathsheba, and she became with child, David ordered that Uriah be put at the forefront of the hottest battle until he was slain. (2 Samuel 11)

Valiant men fought for Israel and for God under Gideon (Judges 7:1), Saul (1 Samuel 14:52), David (2 Samuel 11:16), and other leaders.

Workers for the kingdom of God like Gaius are commended by Paul as "fellow workers for the truth." (3 John 1:1-8)

Xerxes, known as Artaxerxes and Ahasuerus, reigned in Persia in the capital of Shushan. His marriage to Queen Esther and her subsequent bravery resulted in the thwarting of a plot by evil Haman to kill the Jews. (Esther)

Young men who had spied on the city of Jericho and were saved by Rahab, were sent in by Joshua before he destroyed the city, to bring out Rahab and all her relatives. (Joshua 6:22-23)

Zacharias served as priest in Judah. During his time to burn incense, the angel Gabriel appeared and told him that he and Elizabeth would have a son in their old age, and to name the son John. (Luke 1:5-22)

"But without faith it is impossible to please Him,..." (Hebrews 11:6)

Musical Instruments from A to Z

"Then David and all the house of Israel played music before the Lord on all kinds of instruments of fir wood, on harps, on stringed instruments, on tambourines, on sistrums, and on cymbals." (2 Samuel 6:5)

Accordion, **A**utoharp

Bass guitar, **B**assoon

Clarinet, **C**ornet, **C**ello, **C**ymbals

Drums, **D**jembe

Electric Piano

Flute, **F**rench Horn

Grand Piano

Harp, **H**armonica

Inci (Philippine bamboo flute)

Jew's Harp, also known as Juice Harp or Jaw Harp

Keyboard

Lyre

Mandolin

Nose Flute

Organ

Piccolo

Quinticlave

Recorder

Saxophone

Trombone, **T**rumpet, **T**ambourine

Ukulele
Violin
Woodwinds
Xylophone
Yehu (wind instrument in China)
Zither

"Thus all Israel brought up the ark of the covenant of the Lord with shouting and with the sound of the horn, with trumpets and with cymbals, making music with stringed instruments and harps."
(1 Chronicles 15:28)

My Favorite Animals and Reasons They Are from A to Z

"So God created great sea creatures and every living thing that moves, with which the waters abounded, according to their kind, and every winged bird according to its kind. And God saw that it was good." (Genesis 1:21)

"And God made the beast of the earth according to its kind, cattle according to its kind, and everything that creeps on the earth according to its kind. And God saw that it was good." (Genesis 1:25)

For years, animals of all kinds have intrigued me. Growing up I had seven pets at once, enjoying each one. God created some wonderful creatures. Animals that have special places in my life are my favorites from A to Z.

African Jumping Frogs came to our family from a family on my church bus route. We accepted the strange gift and enjoyed them for a few months until they "jumped" out of their bowl and disappeared.

Black bears paced in a cage atop Clinch Mountain, Tennessee, while we vacationers stopped to visit and admire them.

Cows charm me because my daddy told me, when we traveled in the mountains, that the cows there had two long legs and two short legs so they could stand on the side of the mountain. Granddaddy's cows at his farm had four legs the same length and he named every one of them Bessie.

Dogs are so loyal. BeeBee listened patiently while I preached to him from my daddy's Bible when I was four. We inherited Skippy when my great-granddaddy Papa John died and no one else would take him. I always felt a little sorry for Skippy because no one really wanted him, not even us, but my dear father would not let Skippy be without a home.

Elephants remind me of the circuses I attended as a little girl and of those to which we took our children. They look majestic and huge with girls riding on their broad backs.

Field mice capture everyone's hearts in stories, cartoons, and movies. They are pictured as cute and friendly.

Goats make me smile. Our neighborhood kids hopped on our bikes after school many afternoons to ride about a mile to ogle at a three-legged billy goat. We thought that was a great adventure.

Hyenas make my favorites list because my loud laugh makes me think I sound like a laughing hyena.

Iguanas when cared for can recognize their owners, eat out of their owners' hands, and become affectionate pets.

June bugs sound like bumblebees on warm summer nights. Mother and I would catch them and watch them walk across the leaf we held. Their shiny green wings looked iridescent.

Kittens have been a part of my life since I can remember. From Puff when I was five to Dream Don gave me for my seventy-second birthday, and the many kittens between, I've loved each one.

Lions are known as the king of the jungle, and my favorite lions are in two separate places. One is Lion who finds his courage in The Wizard of Oz. The other lions I read about over and over are in a den with Daniel. God sent an angel to shut the mouths of the lions to save Daniel. (Daniel 6:22)

Monkeys show me happiness. I still have the stuffed monkey my classmate Billy gave me for Christmas in the eighth grade. His smile never diminishes.

Newts are scientifically a kind of salamander that is semiaquatic. In my everyday life, newts are little creatures that I cannot decipher from lizards.

Otters have such cute and adorable faces. They are extremely active, playful, curious, and social.

Ponies are animals that most children wish they had. I have a picture that a traveling photographer took of me when I was eight, sitting on a pony in my front yard. Don begged his parents for a pony that he knew he could keep under their high back porch.

Quokkas are known as "the happiest animals on earth." A quokka is a furry mammal whose face forms a perpetual smile. People try to take selfies with quokkas because the little animals look so pleasant. They live on islands off of western Australia.

Rabbits hop in our yards and can become a nuisance for our gardens. I had a pet rabbit once. Daddy brought cabbage and lettuce leaves from his grocery store to feed him. As I grew older, I tired of feeding the rabbit and felt sorry for him in a cage. We gave him to Uncle Cleve who told me he ate him!!

Salmon are born in fresh water, swim to the ocean, then return to fresh water to spawn, most of them returning to where they were born. Pictures of salmon leaping from the water as they swim upstream against strong currents, some for hundreds of miles, inspire me.

Tigers look elegant and stately and walk softly on large, padded feet. Tigers in my life have been stuffed toys, behind the fence of a zoo, or mascots for athletic teams.

Unicorn is the translation used in the King James Version of the Bible for the Hebrew word *reym*. Modern translations used the term "wild ox." Unicorns are mentioned in the Old Testament nine times. They are described as strong (Numbers 23:22; 24:8) and horned (Deuteronomy 33:17; Psalm 92:10). Unicorns of the Bible are extinct, long-horned, ancestors of domestic cattle and have NOTHING to do with the mythical horned horse of cartoons and movies.

Vicunas live mainly in Peru, but also in other South American countries. They are relatives to alpacas and llamas, but their temperament will not let them be domesticated. Their fleece is soft, long, and luscious so fibers made from it are then made into expensive coats and capes.

Walruses socialize readily and can be easily recognized by their tusks, flippers, and whiskers. I have enjoyed seeing trained walruses in water shows and like to hear them bellow.

Xerus is a type of ground squirrel found in Africa. I am using this animal to say squirrels are animals I like to watch in my backyard. They chase each other around trees and scoot here and there.

Yaks are oxlike mammals that I have seen only in zoos. They are usually pictured in children's alphabet books as the word starting with Y.

Zebras each have unique black and white stripes and are beautiful animals. Though they are in the horse family, they are not domesticated.

"For every beast of the forest is Mine, And the cattle on a thousand hills." (Psalm 50:10)

My Thoughts Concerning Vacations
from A to Z

The Bible does not use the word "vacation," but it does talk about "rest." God rested from his work after creation. Part of a vacation is to rest from the labors of our ordinary days. In Mark 6:31 when Jesus' disciples had been so busy they did not have time to eat, Jesus told them, "Come aside by yourselves to a deserted place and rest a while."

When I was growing up, my family took a vacation one week each year. We made plans to drive to sites we could reach, visit, and drive home within the week. From Eastern North Carolina we visited the mountains and the coast. Within our reach were Niagara Falls, New York City, Washington D. C., Virginia mountains, Florida, Rock City, Blowing Rock, Grandfather's Mountain, and a Major League Baseball game in Cincinnati. Little phrases that pop into my mind about vacations are:

Always looked forward to
Better with family
Counted as special times
Do not come often enough
Exciting
Fun
Good for health
Happy times
Intended to be a break from everyday activities

Jelly and peanut butter sandwiches for lunch

Known to bring on merriment

Learning history from visiting places is possible.

Making memories

Needed

Out of routine, something different

Preparations can be laborious

Quiet and restful times

Relaxing

Stressful when we get lost

Time of refreshing

Used to teach Vacation Bible School or go on a mission trip

Very looked forward to

Worth all the effort and money

eXpensive

Yearly for many people

Zip by and end too quickly

Three cheers for vacations!!

*Come unto me, all ye that labour and are heavy laden,
and I will give you rest. (Matthew 11:28)*

My Thoughts on Aging from A to Z

Society today does not seem to value the aged. We joke about our physical weaknesses, our prescriptions, and our "senior moments." In Scripture God used old men and women to do great things for Him. Caleb brought the spy report of Canaan at forty, and received his inheritance at eighty-five. (Joshua 14:10) Abraham was one hundred and Sarah was ninety when Isaac was born. (Genesis 17:17) Moses and Aaron spoke to Pharoah at the ages of eighty and eighty-three. (Exodus 7:7)

Luke 1:7 tells us Zacharias and Elizabeth "were both well advanced in years" when God gave them John. Life holds much anticipation as the years pass. The following thoughts come to my mind concerning aging.

Anna, a widow for 84 years living in the temple in Jerusalem (Luke 2:36-38), and Simeon, a "just and devout" man living in the town (Luke 2:25-32), were privileged in their old age to witness their Redeemer and Promised One. I am looking for the return of that same One (Acts 1:11), and what a privilege it would be to see His coming!!

Be thankful for each birthday! We could have already passed from this world. I am Blessed beyond measure. I say with David, "'Who am I, O Lord God? And what is my house, that You have brought me this far?'" (2 Samuel 7:18)

Children I punished and disciplined now tell me they understand. How rewarding to see them correct and guide their children.

Driving isn't as fun. I am more conscious of danger.

Eyesight fails. I'm afraid I am more like Isaac who "was old and his eyes were dim" (Genesis 27:1) than Moses who, when he died at 120, "His eyes were not dim nor his natural vigor diminished." (Deuteronomy 34:7)

Falling is a fear. I know too many friends who break bones and have terrible injuries.

Grandchildren are a delight! "Children's children are the crown of old men,..." (Proverbs 17:6)

Health is in my thoughts more often. Doctors' appointments are more frequent.

Importance placed on material things diminishes. However, some items get more sentimental.

Jesus will never leave me nor forsake me. (Hebrews 13:5)

Keeping up with changes around me is hard, but needful, so I try to stay aware of what young people are facing.

Listening to younger people is important. My doctors, dentist, pastor, hair dresser, and mechanic are much younger than I.

Memories become more precious. "Only take heed to yourself, and diligently keep yourself, lest you forget the things your eyes have seen, and lest they depart from your heart all the days of your life. And teach them to your children and your grandchildren," (Deuteronomy 4:9)

No circumstance I face keeps the sun from coming up or going down.

Others' situations become more real because I am able to identify since I have had more problems.

Prayer is vital! "pray without ceasing," (1 Thessalonians 5:17)

Quietness is sweeter. "In quietness and confidence shall be your strength." (Isaiah 30:15)

Regardless of circumstances, God is in control. "The Lord reigns; Let the earth rejoice;" (Psalm 97:1)

Strength for each day is available. "As your days, so shall your strength be." (Deuteronomy 33:25b)

Truth is still absolute even if many people do not believe it is.

Usefulness to family and society does not disappear. Tasks I perform may change, but I can still be encouraging in different ways.

Volunteering is a way to stay active and helpful to others.

Wisdom comes with age is a saying I've heard since I was young. I hope through experience that the adage is true.

e**X**tended time is needed for naps.

Young people are a delight to watch grow older. For example, the young adults at church who sing, teach the little ones to sing. The youth from years past are now the deacons, teachers, and leaders of the church.

Zephaniah 3:17 is a great comfort. "The Lord your God in your midst, The Mighty One, will save; He will rejoice over you with gladness, He will quiet you with His love, He will rejoice over you with singing."

"The righteous shall flourish like a palm tree, He shall grow like a cedar in Lebanon. Those who are planted in the house of the LORD Shall flourish in the courts of our God. They shall still bear fruit in old age; They shall be fresh and flourishing, To declare that the LORD is upright; He is my rock, and there is no unrighteousness in Him."
(Psalm 92:12-15)

My Thoughts on Vegetable Gardening
from A to Z

"And the earth brought forth grass, the herb that yields seed according to its kind, and the tree that yields fruit, whose seed is in itself according to its kind. And God saw that it was good." (Genesis 1:12)

Almanac instructions and schedule for planting works.

Beans know to grow up the strings between the poles marking the row.

Corn does not grow well in my husband Don's garden.

Drought reduces the production of the garden.

Energy is needed to work in a garden.

Fertilizer enhances the production of the garden.

Gardening gives a sense of accomplishment.

Hard work is involved in growing a garden, but getting to eat the delicious vegetables is worth the effort.

Irrigation can be necessary in dry weather.

Juxtapositioning types of plants make a difference in their growth and fruit bearing.

Keeping up with weeding and watering are monumental tasks.

Ladybugs eat up to 50 aphids a day, being helpful as a pest control for gardens.

Morning glories look lovely throughout the bean vines.

Never wear short sleeves to pick beans. The itch afterwards is unpleasant.

Overplanting in one area is not helpful. Thinning the plants is necessary.

Produce from the garden tastes fresh and delicious.

Quit work before the sun makes the day too hot. Work early in the morning and in the evening.

Roots need room to grow, so plant giving them space.

Seeds best to be saved to plant next year come from self-pollinating crops like beans, peas, peppers, and tomatoes.

Too much rain makes roots rot.

Undertaking the responsibility of growing a garden is a huge commitment of time.

Vegetables from the garden taste better than vegetables shipped to a store.

Weeds grow faster than the food plants.

eXtreme heat dries up the plants and soil.

Yearly tasks such as tilling and fertilizing need to be done to prepare the soil.

Zinnias planted in a vegetable garden look beautiful and attract cross-pollinators.

"Their souls shall be like a well-watered garden, And they shall sorrow no more at all." (Jeremiah 31:12)

Noted in the Bible as Precious from A to Z

We refer to babies and tiny pets as precious. An old hymn "Precious Memories" recalls how meaningful people and events can be in our lives. The Bible refers to a variety of items, some tangible and some intangible, as precious. Look for what you would consider precious from A to Z.

Articles of gold and silver (Daniel 11:8)

Blood of Christ (1 Peter 1:18-19)

Children of Israel (Micah 1:16)

Death of a saint (Psalm 116:15)

Every precious thing in God's sight (Job 28:5-11)

Fruit of the earth (James 5:7)

Genuineness of your faith (1 Peter 1:6-7)

His lovingkindness (Psalm 36:7)

Israel (Isaiah 43:3-4)

Jewelry and clothing (Genesis 24:53)

King Jesus (1 Peter 2:7)

Life (Psalm 22:19-20; 35:17-18)

Monthly produce of the land (Deuteronomy 33:13-15)

Needy saved souls' blood (Psalm 72:13-14)

Oil (Psalm 133:1-2)

Promises (2 Peter 1:4)

Quiet spirit (1 Peter 3:4)

Riches (Proverbs 24:3-4)

Stones in the foundation of New Jerusalem (Revelation 21:19)

Things of Egypt (Daniel 11:43)

Understanding and wisdom (Proverbs 3:13-19)

Vessels (Jeremiah 25:34; Ezra 8:27)

Wood of Babylon (Revelation 18:11-12)

eXceptional blessings given by Moses to the descendants of Joseph (Deuteronomy 33:13-17)

Your thoughts to me, O God (Psalms 139:17)

Zion's sons (Lamentations 4:2)

"Therefore thus says the Lord God: 'Behold, I lay in Zion a stone for a foundation, A tried stone, a precious cornerstone, a sure foundation; Whoever believes will not act hastily.'" (Isaiah 28:16)

O Lord, Give Me...from A to Z

"And Solomon said to God:...'Now give me wisdom and knowledge,...'"
(2 Chronicles 1:8, 10)

My husband Don's favorite contemporary Christian song is "Where I Belong" by Building 429. A line in the chorus says "Take this world and give me Jesus...,"acknowledging his desire to put Jesus first in his life. Anne Graham Lotz titled a book she wrote *Just Give Me Jesus*. Her devotions are accompanied by the music of Fernando Ortega as he sings "Give Me Jesus." As we strive to be more like Jesus, we can look to the examples of people who showed qualities we admire.

O Lord, please give me:

Actions like Dorcas. (Acts 9:36-41)

Belief like Abraham. (Hebrews 11:8-10; Genesis 12:1-5)

Courage like Daniel. (Daniel 6:4-22)

Daring like David's three mighty men. (1 Chronicles 11:15-20)

Encouragement like Barnabus. (Acts 15:24-29)

Faith like Joseph. (Hebrews 11:22; Genesis 50:24)

Guidance like the Wise Men from the East. (Matthew 2:1-11)

Heart like David. (1 Samuel 13:13-14; Acts 13:22)

Intercession like Elijah. (James 5:16-18; 1 Kings 17:1; 1 Kings 18)

Judgment like Nathan. (2 Samuel 12:1-15)

Knowledge like Phillip. (Acts 8:26-38)

Leadership like Moses. (Psalm 77:20; Exodus 6:26-27;

Exodus 12:40-43; Exodus 14:13-16; Deuteronomy 34:10; Isaiah 63:11-12)

Missionary Spirit like Paul. (Acts 13:1-2)

Nurturing like Jochebed. (Numbers 26:59; Exodus 2:1-9)

Obedience like Gideon. (Judges 7:13-25)

Patience like Job. (Job 1:13-22; Job 2:1-10)

Quietness like Mary, mother of Jesus. (Luke 2:19)

Rest like Jehoshaphat. (2 Chronicles 20:1-30)

Strength like Samson. (Judges 16:4-22, 25-30)

Trust like Rahab. (Joshua 2:1-21; Joshua 6:22-25; Hebrews 11:31)

Understanding like the Bereans. (Acts 17:10-12)

Victory like Joshua. (Exodus 17:13; Deuteronomy 3:28, 34:9; Book of Joshua)

Wisdom like Solomon. (1 Kings 3:16-28, 4:29-34; 2 Chronicles 1:7-12)

eXcitement like the man Peter and John healed. (Acts 3:1-10)

Yearning to see people saved and healed like the four friends who brought their friend to Jesus. (Mark 2:1-12)

Zeal like Peter. (John 21:1-19)

"I will never forget Your precepts, For by them You have given me life."
(Psalm 119:93)

Outstanding Women of the Bible from A to Z

Who can find a virtuous woman? For her price is far above rubies.
(Proverbs 31:10 KJV)

Women during the time of the Old Testament were under the complete authority of either their fathers or their husbands. Passages tell of fathers giving daughters to men and husbands putting away wives. (Genesis 29:21-28; Deuteronomy 24:1) However, some women held respected positions. Deborah was a judge and prophetess. (Judges 4:4-5) The Queen of Sheba was quite influential. (1 Kings 10:1-13) The daughters of Zelophehad stood to ask Moses for the inheritance of their father since he had no sons. (Numbers 27:1-8)

Jesus lifted the value of women greatly in His time on earth. Women ministered to Jesus as they followed as disciples. (Luke 8:1-3) Jesus performed miracles for women, and used them as examples of faith. (Luke 7:11-15; Matthew 8:14-15; Mark 7:25-29; Mark 12:41-44; Matthew 12:20-22) Almost two hundred names of women appear in the Bible. There appear outstanding women from A to Z.

Abigail, with her wisdom and generosity, prevented David from killing her rude husband Nabal and his household. God took Nabal's life and David took beautiful Abigail as his wife. (1 Samuel 25:2-42)
Bilhah, Rachel's maid, bore Jacob two sons, Dan and Naphtali (Genesis 29:29; 30:1-8)
Candace, Queen of Ethiopia, sent her man in charge of her treasury to Jerusalem where he heard about Jesus, and on his way home was met by Philip who explained Scripture to him and baptized him. (Acts 8:26-38)

Deborah judged Israel, rode into battle with Barak to defeat Jabin king of Canaan, and God gave Israel rest from war for forty years. (Judges 4-5)

Esther, queen and wife of King Ahasuerus, bravely approached her husband to expose the plot of Haman to destroy her people the Jews. The king listened to Esther, allowed the Jews to defend themselves, and they soundly defeated their enemies. (Esther 1-10)

Felix's wife Drusilla, a Jew, joined her husband the Roman governor of Judea to listen to Paul explain the good news of Jesus Christ. Sadly, neither Felix nor Drusilla accepted the claims of Christ. (Acts 24:24-25)

Gomer was a woman of harlotry that God told Hosea to take as a wife. Her unfaithfulness to Hosea gave a picture to Israel of their unfaithfulness to God. Hosea cast her out in anger, then God told Hosea to buy Gomer back for himself to show how God would bring Israel back to Himself. (Hosea 1:3; 2:2-3; 3:1-2)

Hannah prayed fervently for a son and told God she would give the child back to Him. God gave her Samuel who, after he was weaned, stayed at the temple with Eli the priest. Hannah brought him a new coat every year. (1 Samuel 1:9-28; 2:18-19)

Iscah was Abram's niece. Her father Haran died in the land of Ur. (Genesis 11:29)

Jezebel worshipped Baal and convinced her evil husband King Ahab to do the same. The wicked woman massacred the Lord's prophets and sought to kill Elijah. Elijah prophesied that dogs would eat the flesh of the immoral queen and they did! (1 Kings 16:31-33; 18:13; 19:1-3; 21:23-25; 2 Kings 9:30-37)

Keturah married Abraham after the death of Sarah. She gave Abraham many sons. (Genesis 25: 1-4)

Lydia heard Paul and Silas as they talked with the women who were gathered by the riverside at Philippi to pray. She was a seller of purple from Thyatira, who worshiped God. She and her household were baptized and insisted that Paul and Silas stay at her home. After God released Paul and Silas from prison, they went to Lydia's to encourage those meeting there. (Acts 16:13-15, 40)

Mary was told by Gabriel that she would be the mother of God's Son, the Messiah. She followed the ministry of Jesus, watched at the foot of His cross as He died, and after Jesus' ascension continued with the disciples. (Luke 1:26-33; 2:4-7; John 2:5; Matthew 12:46; John 19:25; Acts 1:14)

Naomi became a widow while in Moab to escape a famine in Judah. Her daughters-in-law, Orpah and Ruth, were Moabitesses. Naomi return to Judah with Ruth and a kinsman redeemer Boaz looked after them. (Ruth 1-4)

Orpah, a Moabitess, married Naomi and Elimelech's son Chilion. After her husband's and sons' deaths, Naomi went back to Judah, and Orpah chose to stay in Moab with her family. (Ruth 1:4-5, 11-14; 4:10)

Priscilla and her husband Aquila met Paul in Corinth, and because they were tentmakers with him, Paul stayed in their home. They traveled to Ephesus with Paul, and stayed there when Paul left. They mentored, taught, and encouraged Apollos in his preaching. A church met in their home. (Acts 18:1-3, 18-19, 24-26; Romans 16:3; 1 Corinthians 16:19)

Queen of Sheba heard of Solomon's fame and came to ask him hard questions. She was impressed with his wisdom and what he built. She brought Solomon great quantities of gold, spices, and gemstones. Solomon reciprocated with generosity before she returned to her home. New Testament writers call her Queen of the South. (1 Kings 10:1-13; 2 Chronicles 9:1-12; Matthew 12:42; Luke 11:31)

Ruth left Moab to be with her mother-in-law Naomi in Judah. There she met and married Boaz, a kinsman redeemer for her dead husband Mahlon. Ruth is listed in the genealogy of Jesus. (Ruth 1-4; Matthew 1:5)

Sarah, Sarai before God changed her name, was beautiful but barren. God appeared to her husband Abraham, who laughed when God told him Sarah would bare a son at ninety years old. Listening from the tent, Sarah laughed also. A year later her son Isaac was born. (Genesis 11:29-30; 12:11; 17:15-17; 18:10-15; 21:1-2)

Tabitha, also translated Dorcas, lived in Joppa. She was a disciple in the early church who made coats and tunics to give to people as good deeds. Tabitha became ill and died. Her friends sent for Peter, who raised her to life. (Acts 9:36-41)

Uriah's wife, Bathsheba, went to King David when he called for her. That meeting resulted in the birth of a child who died. David ordered Uriah killed in battle, then married Bathsheba. They later became parents to Solomon. (2 Samuel 11:2-5, 14-17, 27; 12:14-19, 24)

Vashti, wife of King Ahasuerus who reigned over one hundred twenty-seven provinces from India to Ethiopia, refused to obey the king to show off her beauty to the king's party-goers. Consequently she was taken out of her position and never allowed to come before the king again. (Esther 1:1-22)

Woman at the well in the city of Sychar in Samaria found Living Water offered to her by Jesus. She told others in the town about meeting the Messiah. Jesus stayed with them two days and many believed on Him. (John 4:5-42)

eXamples of faithful women ministered to Jesus as he traveled from town to town. Among them were Joanna, Susanna, Mary Magdalene, and many others who cared for Him out of their own resources. (Luke 8:1-3)

Young servant girl from Israel had been captured by Naaman, the commander of the army for the king of Syria. Naaman was a leper, and the young servant girl told Naaman's wife that there was a prophet in Israel who could ask the God of Israel to heal Naaman's leprosy. She knew her God was the True God. Naaman went to Elisha and God did heal him. (2 Kings 5:1-14)

Zipporah married Moses while he lived in Midian with the family of her father Jethro. She and their two sons, Gershom and Eliezer, left with Moses to go to Egypt. At some point, Moses sent Zipporah and their sons back to her home, because Jethro brought them back to Moses after the Exodus. I think Moses knew his family would be in danger in Egypt. (Exodus 2:16-18, 21-22; 3:1; 4:19-20; 18:1-7)

"Then the rib which the LORD God had taken from man He made into a woman, and He brought her to the man. And Adam said: 'This is now bone of my bones And flesh of my flesh; She shall be called Woman, Because she was taken out of Man.'" (Genesis 2:22-23)

People Jesus Encountered from A to Z

"...He went through every city and village, preaching and bringing the glad tidings of the kingdom of God...." (Luke 8:1)

Anna, a widow who stayed in the temple in Jerusalem to pray, was present when Jesus' parents brought Him to be presented to the Lord. (Luke 2:36-38)

Bartimaeus, a blind man, sat by the road begging. He cried out to Jesus for healing and was made whole. (Mark 10:46-52)

Children were brought to Jesus, and He took them in His arms, and blessed them. (Mark 10:13-16; Luke 18:15-17)

Deaf came to Jesus and were made to hear. (Mark 7:31-37)

Eager ones pressed into the crowd where Jesus spoke, and He healed many. (Mark 3:20)

Fishermen left their boats to follow Jesus. (Matthew 4: 21-22)

Governor Pontius Pilate wished to release Jesus, but instead delivered Him to the chief priests, the rulers, and the people. (Luke 23:13-25)

High Priest Caiaphas sent Jesus to the Praetorium and to Pilate in the early morning. (John 18:28)

Ill, mute, and lame were included in the multitudes that came to Jesus to be healed. (Matthew 15:30-31)

Joseph of Arimathea courageously asked Pilate for the body of Jesus. (Mark 15:43)

King Herod had beheaded John the Baptist. When he heard about the things Jesus did, Herod thought surely John the Baptist had come back from the dead. (Mark 6:14)

Lazarus died and was buried four days before Jesus arrived to call him forth from the grave. (John 11:14-44)

Mary and Martha, sisters who lived in the village of Bethany, hosted Jesus in their home. (Luke 10:38-42)

Nicodemus, a Pharisee and ruler of the Jews, came to Jesus by night and learned he needed a spiritual birth. (John 3:1-7) He brought spices and helped Joseph of Arimathea wrap and prepare Jesus' body for burial. (John 19:38-40)

One who was paralyzed and lying on a bed was brought to Jesus, who not only gave him spiritual healing, but also told him to take up his bed and go to his house. The multitudes marveled when they saw this miracle. (Matthew 9:1-8)

Peter left his fishing boat to follow Jesus (Matthew 4:28-20), denied knowing Jesus (Matthew 26: 69-75), but became strong in preaching the gospel. (Acts 2:36-39)

Questioners followed Jesus, trying to trap Him to bring charges against him. (Matthew 22:15-17)

Rich young ruler came to Jesus asking how to have eternal life. (Luke 18:18-23)

Simeon, a just and devout man, was prompted by the Holy Spirit to go to the temple to see the Child who was to be the Light to the Gentiles and the Glory of Israel. (Luke 2:25-32)

Thomas doubted Jesus appeared to the other disciples until Jesus let him feel His wounds. (John 20:24-29)

Unclean lepers stood far from Jesus and cried for mercy. Jesus healed them. (Luke 17:11-19)

Vipers is the word Jesus used to describe the Pharisees who thought of themselves as more righteous than others. (Matthew 12:34)

Woman at the well in Samaria became a missionary to those in her town when she met Jesus, who offered her Living Water. (John 4:5-42)

eXtended family of Jesus included his cousin John the Baptist. (Luke 1:13-17, 26-41)

Young described the man lying dead and being taken out of the city of Nain. His mother, a widow, wept for her only son. Jesus had compassion and raised the young man. (Luke 7:11-15)

Zacchaeus, a rich tax collector in Jericho, climbed a tree to see Jesus, who visited Zacchaeus in his home, and brought salvation to him. (Luke 19:1-10)

"And when He had come into Jerusalem, all the city was moved, saying, 'Who is this?'" (Matthew 21:10)

Places Jesus Went from A to Z

"Wherever He entered, into villages, cities, or the country, they laid the sick in the marketplaces, and begged Him that they might just touch the hem of His garment. And as many as touched Him were made well."
(Mark 6:56)

Aside—"Then He took the twelve aside and said to them, 'Behold, we are going up to Jerusalem,...'" (Luke 18:31)

Bethany—"Then, six days before the Passover, Jesus came to Bethany, where Lazarus was who had been dead, whom He had raised from the dead."(John 12:1)

Capernaum—"Then they went into Capernaum, and immediately on the Sabbath He entered the synagogue and taught." (Mark 1:21)

Deserted place—"Now when it was day, He departed and went into a deserted place. And the crowd sought Him and came to Him,…"
(Luke 4:42)

Egypt—"When he (Joseph) arose, he took the young Child and His mother by night and departed for Egypt,…" (Matthew 2:14)

Fields—"At that time Jesus went through the grainfields on the Sabbath. And His disciples were hungry, and began to pluck heads of grain and to eat." (Matthew 12:1)

Galilee—"And Jesus went about all Galilee, teaching in their synagogues, preaching the gospel of the kingdom, and healing all kinds of sickness and all kinds of disease among the people." (Matthew 4:23)

Heaven—"And while they looked steadfastly toward heaven as He went up, behold, two men stood by them in white apparel, who also said,

'Men of Galilee, why do you stand gazing up into heaven? This same Jesus, who was taken up from you into heaven, will so come in like manner as you saw Him go into heaven.'" (Acts 1:10-11)

Israel—"Then he (Joseph) arose, took the young Child and His mother, and came into the land of Israel." (Matthew 2:21)

Jerusalem—"Then He took the twelve aside and said to them, 'Behold, we are going up to Jerusalem, and all things that are written by the prophets concerning the Son of Man will be accomplished.' (Luke 18:31)

Kidron—"When Jesus had spoken these words, He went out with His disciples over the Brook Kidron, where there was a garden, which He and His disciples entered. (John 18:1)

Lake Gennesaret—"So it was, as the multitude pressed about Him to hear the word of God, that He stood by the Lake of Gennesaret," (Luke 5:1)

Mount of Olives—"Coming out, He went to the Mount of Olives, as He was accustomed, and His disciples also followed Him." (Luke 22:39)

Nazareth—"It came to pass in those days that Jesus came from Nazareth of Galilee, and was baptized by John in the Jordan." (Mark 1:9)

Out—"On the same day Jesus went out of the house and sat by the sea." (Matthew 13:1)

Praetorium—"Then the soldiers of the governor took Jesus into the Praetorium and gathered the whole garrison around Him." (Matt 27:27)

Quiet place—"…He departed again to the mountain by Himself alone." (John 6:15)

Road to Emmaus—"Now behold, two of them were traveling that same day to a village called Emmaus, which was seven miles from Jerusalem. And they talked together of all these things which had happened. So it was, while they conversed and reasoned, that Jesus Himself drew near and went with them. (Luke 24:13-15)

Samaria—"So He came to a city of Samaria which is called Sychar, near the plot of ground that Jacob gave to his son Joseph. (John 4:5)

Temple—"Now when He came into the temple, the chief priests and the elders of the people confronted Him as He was teaching, and said, 'By what authority are You doing these things? And who gave You this authority?'" (Matthew 21:23)

Upper room—"Then you shall say to the master of the house, 'The Teacher says to you, "Where is the guest room where I may eat the Passover with My disciples?" Then he will show you a large, furnished upper room; there make ready.' So they went and found it just as He had said to them, and they prepared the Passover. When the hour had come, He sat down, and the twelve apostles with Him." (Luke 22:11-14)

Villages—"And He went through the cities and villages, teaching, and journeying toward Jerusalem." (Luke 13:22)

Wedding—"…there was a wedding in Cana of Galilee, and the mother of Jesus was there. Now both Jesus and His disciples were invited to the wedding." (John 2:1-2)

eXpedient places to minister—"Then His fame went throughout all Syria; and they brought to Him all sick people who were afflicted with various diseases and torments, and those who were demon-possessed, epileptics, and paralytics; and He healed them." (Matthew 4:24)

Yearly feasts—"Now on the first day of the Feast of the Unleavened Bread the disciples came to Jesus, saying to Him, 'Where do You want us to prepare for You to eat the Passover?'" (Matthew 26:17). "Now the Jews' Feast of Tabernacles was at hand. But when His brothers had gone up, then He also went up to the feast, not openly, but as it were in secret." (John 7:2, 10)

Zaccheus' house—"And when Jesus came to the place, He looked up and saw him, and said to him, 'Zacchaeus, make haste and come down, for today I must stay at your house.'" (Luke 19:5)

"Now it came to pass, afterward, that He went through every city and village, preaching and bringing the glad tidings of the kingdom of God."
(Luke 8:1)

Praise the Lord for Conveniences
from A to Z

"Now godliness with contentment is great gain. For we brought nothing into this world, and it is certain we can carry nothing out. And having food and clothing, with these we shall be content." (1 Timothy 6:6-8)

We enjoy much in our way of life that is actually unnecessary for life itself. We desire more than necessities and we are thankful for conveniences. Praise the Lord for…

Automobiles. I don't think I would travel well on a horse.

Bathrooms. I used an outhouse when I visited my grandparents as a little girl.

Cell phones. I grew up without one, but now I think it is indispensible.

Dishwashers. Definitely not a need, but how I enjoy this appliance in my kitchen.

Electricity. Flipping a switch for lights, cooking, and heat is almost taken for granted.

Fast food. Sometimes a quick, already cooked meal fits the occasion.

Garages. When it is raining and I am able to walk out my door and enter a dry car, I am pleased.

Hairdryers. They make getting ready for the day easier and faster.

Ice cream sandwiches. Delicious ice cream without even dipping or messing up a dish.

Jumper cables. I've left my car lights on too many times.

Keyboards that delete with a backspace key. When I typed research papers for Don and me in college and seminary on a typewriter, correcting mistakes was much tougher.

Laser light shows. How entertaining to watch the displays that seem magic.

Microwaves. Years ago, Don thought we didn't need one. Now we use it every day.

Nutella®. Some people who are allergic to peanuts can eat Nutella®.

Online shopping. Buying items from my recliner is super easy.

Plumbing and **P**aved roads. Turning on a faucet to have water is so simple. The street where I lived growing up turned to mud when rain came. My family's car got stuck many times.

Quick grits. Corn already ground, packaged and quickly cooked makes good eating.

Radios. I marvel at hearing voices and music from far away.

Stadium seats. I like comfort.

Televisions. In several rooms in our home, I watch, in color, entertainment, news, and sports.

Umbrellas. I use this small canopy during rain or sun.

Velcro. What a delightful way to hold items together!

Watches. Telling times is important almost every day.

X-rays. Being able to look inside the human body to help diagnose and treat medical problems aids each of us.

Yearbooks. I look at those pictures of young schoolmates with happiness and smiles.

Zippers. The gaps left by buttons or safety pins are filled with these tiny continuous teeth.

"Anyone who wants to follow me must put aside his own desires and conveniences and carry his cross with him every day and keep close to me!" (Luke 9:23 TLB)

Prayer Is ... from A to Z

"Evening and morning and at noon I will pray, and cry aloud, And He shall hear my voice." (Psalm 55:17)

Prayer is:

Asking.

Believing.

Confessing.

Deliberate.

Enveloping.

Finding God's heart.

Guidance from Him.

Honoring.

Interceding.

Joy.

Knowing God better.

Listening.

Making desires known.

Near to His heart.

Opening our hearts to Him.

Persisting.

Questioning.

Receiving.

Specific.

Thanksgiving.

Uniting our hearts with His.

Visualizing things that are not so they might become.

Waiting.

e**X**tending our will to meet His.

Yielding my will in asking for His.

Zoning in on His desires for me.

"In this manner, therefore, pray: Our Father in heaven, hallowed
be Your name. Your kingdom come. Your will be done on earth
as it is in heaven. Give us this day our daily bread.
And forgive us our debts, as we forgive our debtors.
And do not lead us into temptation, but deliver us from the evil one.
For Yours is the kingdom and the power and the glory forever. Amen."
(Matthew 6:9-13)

Praying for Oneself from A to Z

" 'Call to Me, and I will answer you, and show you
great and mighty things, which you do not know.' "(Jeremiah 33:3)

Dear Father,

Your Word tells us that You hear us when we pray. We pray for others and we know we need to pray for ourselves so we can stay strong in Your strength. Our cries span from A to Z.

Answer me, O Lord. "Give ear, O LORD, to my prayer; And attend to the voice of my supplications. In the day of my trouble I will call upon You, For You will answer me." (Psalm 86:6-7)

Bless me, O Lord. "The Lord will give strength to His people; The Lord will bless His people with peace." (Psalm 29:11)

Cover me with your goodness. "I will greatly rejoice in the Lord, My soul shall be joyful in my God; For He has clothed me with the garments of salvation, He has covered me with the robe of righteousness,…" (Isaiah 61:10)

Deliver me from evil. "And do not lead us into temptation, But deliver us from the evil one. For Yours is the kingdom and the power and the glory forever. Amen." (Matthew 6:13)

Establish me in Your ways. "I pray that out of his glorious riches he may strengthen you with power through his Spirit in your inner being, so that Christ may dwell in your hearts through faith. And I pray that you, being rooted and established in love, may have power, together with all the Lord's holy people, to grasp how wide and long and high and deep is the love of Christ," (Ephesians 3:16-18 NIV)

Feed me just what I need to serve You. "Two things I request of You (Deprive me not before I die): Remove falsehood and lies far from me; Give me neither poverty nor riches—Feed me with the food allotted to me; Lest I be full and deny You, And say, 'Who is the Lord?' Or lest I be poor and steal, And profane the name of my God." (Proverbs 30:7-9)

Grant me pleasure in Your will. "May He grant you according to your heart's desire, And fulfill all your purpose." (Psalm 20:4)

Heal my weak body. "Heal me, O Lord, and I shall be healed; Save me, and I shall be saved, For You are my praise." (Jeremiah 17:14)

Ignite the gift of Your Spirit in me. "For this reason I remind you to fan into flame the gift of God, which is in you through the laying on of my hands." (2 Timothy 1:6 NIV)

Judge my ways to help me improve. "For though I were righteous, I could not answer Him; I would beg mercy of my Judge." (Job 9:15)

Keep me from sin. "And Jabez called on the God of Israel saying, 'Oh, that You would bless me indeed, and enlarge my territory, that Your hand would be with me, and that You would keep me from evil, that I may not cause pain!' So God granted him what he requested."
(1 Chronicles 4:10)

Love me with Your everlasting love. "The Lord has appeared of old to me, saying: 'Yes, I have loved you with an everlasting love;'"
(Jeremiah 31:3)

Mold me into someone You can use to further Your Kingdom. "Remember that you molded me like clay." (Job 10:9 NIV)

Name me as Your child. "But as many as received Him, to them He gave the right to become children of God, to those who believe in His name:" (John 1:12)

Open my eyes to see others as You see them. "And when Jesus went out He saw a great multitude; and He was moved with compassion for them,..." (Matthew 14:14)

Protect me from straying from Your will. "So He said to them, 'When you pray, say: Our Father in heaven, Hallowed be Your name. Your kingdom come. Your will be done On earth as it is in heaven.'"
(Luke 11:2)

Quiet me with Your love. "For thus says the Lord God, the Holy One of Israel: 'In returning and rest you shall be saved; In quietness and confidence shall be your strength.'" (Isaiah 30:15)

Remember my sins no more. "For I will be merciful to their unrighteousness, and their sins and their lawless deeds I will remember no more." (Hebrews 8:12)

Search my heart and lead me. "Search me, O God, and know my heart; Try me, and know my anxieties; And see if there is any wicked way in me, And lead me in the way everlasting." (Psalm 139:23-24)

Teach me Your ways. "You call Me Teacher and Lord, and you say well, for so I am." (John 13:13)

Uphold me when I am weak. "Uphold my steps in Your paths, That my footsteps may not slip." (Psalm 17:5)

Vindicate me by Your strength and Your name. "Save me, O God, by Your name, And vindicate me by Your strength." (Psalm 54:1)

Watch out for me and help me keep my heart loyal to You. "For the eyes of the Lord run to and fro throughout the whole earth, to show Himself strong on behalf of those whose heart is loyal to Him."
(2 Chronicles 16:9)

X-ray my heart and keep me in Your will. "Now He who searches the hearts knows what the mind of the Spirit is, because He makes intercession for the saints according to the will of God." (Romans 8:27)

Yank me from things of the world and draw me close to You. "Yes, I have loved you with an everlasting love; Therefore with lovingkindness I have drawn you." (Jeremiah 31:3)

Zip my lips when needed. "Set a guard, O Lord, over my mouth; Keep watch over the door of my lips." (Psalm 141:3)

"Hear my cry, O God; Attend to my prayer." (Psalm 61:1)

Precious Stones in Our Beautiful World
from A to Z

"And he decorated the house with precious stones for beauty,..."
(2 Chronicles 3:6)

"And you shall put settings of stones in it (breastplate),
four rows of stones: The first row shall be a sardius, a topaz,
and an emerald; this shall be the first row; the second row shall be a
turquoise, a sapphire, and a diamond; the third row, a jacinth,
an agate, and an amethyst; and the fourth row, a beryl, an onyx,
and a jasper. They shall be set in gold settings." (Exodus 28:17-20)

Magnificent gems lie in their hidden habitats all over our scenic planet. Many are mentioned in the Bible. The Hebrew names differ from some of the Greek names of the gems and some names are not clear. They present themselves from A to Z.

Amethyst (Exodus 28:19; 39:12; Revelation 21:20)
Beryl (Ezekiel 28:13; Exodus 28:20; 39:13; Revelation 21:20)
Chalcedony (Revelation 21:19)
Diamond (Ezekiel 28:13; Exodus 28:18; 39:11)
Emerald (Exodus 28:17; 39:10; Revelation 4:3; 21:19)
Fire Agate (kind of chalcedony with iridescent colors) (Exodus 28:19; Exodus 39:12)
Garnet (deep red stone popular in jewelry, the birthstone for January)
Hyacinth (Revelation 9:17) can also be spelled Jacinth. (Exodus 28:19;

39:12; Revelation 21:20)

Iris Agate (Exodus 28:19; 39:12)

Jasper (Exodus 28:20; 39:13; Ezekiel 28:13; Revelation 4:3; 21:11, 18)

Kyanite (a blue mineral found in quartz)

Lapis Lazuli (New Jerusalem Bible translates this stone as the pavement under the feet of God in Exodus 24:9-10)

Moonstone (a popular gem that gets its name because the glow just below the surface of the stone is like looking at the moon through clouds.)

Nephrite (a hard, white or pale green form of jade)

Onyx (Genesis 2:12; Exodus 28:9, 20; 39:6, 13; Ezekiel 28:13)

Pearl (Matthew 13:45-46; Revelation 21:21)

Quartz (Job 28:17-18)

Ruby (Job 28:18; Proverbs 3:15; 8:11; 20:15; 31:10; Ezekiel 27:16)

Sapphire (Exodus 24:10; 28:18; 39:11; Isaiah 54:11; Ezekiel 28:13; Revelation 21:19)

Topaz (Exodus 28:17; 39:10; Job 28:18-19; Ezekiel 28:13; Revelation 21:20)

Unakite (a kind of granite first found in the mountains of North Carolina, is mottled pink and green.)

Variscite (a rare mineral of aluminum phosphate that is usually green and often used to make small sculptures.)

Wonderstone (a kind of jasper found in the United States with pale bands of yellow, tan, maroon, violet, or pink)

eXquisite jewels (Proverbs 20:15; Isaiah 61:10; Zechariah 9:16; Malachi 3:17)

Yacinthos (according to www.gemcoach.com, this stone in the original Koine Greek is in the foundation for the wall in Revelation 21:19-20.)

Zircon (popular gemstone for many years, is the modern birthstone for December. It has the brightness of diamond but is cheaper. It is not cubic zirconium, which is manmade.)

"'They shall be Mine,' says the LORD of hosts, 'On the day that I make them My jewels and I will spare them as a man spares his own son who serves him.'" (Malachi 3:17)

"The construction of its wall was of jasper; and the city was pure gold, like clear glass. The foundations of the wall of the city were adorned with all kinds of precious stones: the first foundation was jasper, the second sapphire, the third chalcedony, the fourth emerald, the fifth sardonyx, the sixth sardius, the seventh chrysolite, the eighth beryl, the ninth topaz, the tenth chrysoprase, the eleventh jacinth, and the twelfth amethyst. The twelve gates were twelve pearls: each individual gate was of one pearl. And the street of the city was pure gold, like transparent glass."
(Revelation 21:18-21)

Reminders of Easter from A to Z

"And He began to teach them that the Son of Man must suffer many things, and be rejected by the elders and chief priests and scribes, and be killed, and after three days rise again." (Mark 8:31)

Atonement was made by Christ for the sins of all people. (1 John 2:2)

Blood sacrifice was necessary. (Hebrews 9:22)

Crucifixion by the Romans was a cruel way to die. (Matthew 20:17-19)

Death of Christ paid for sins. (1 Peter 2:24)

Extreme agony through beatings, being spit upon and a crown of thorns came to Jesus. (John 19:1-3)

Future living in the presence of Christ was given. (John 14:3)

Grave and death were overcome. (Matthew 28:6)

Home in Heaven awaits believers. (John 14:1-6)

Invitation to follow Christ is issued. (Luke 24:45-49)

Joseph of Arimathea took Jesus' body from the cross and placed it in his new tomb. (Matthew 27:57-60)

Kin and friends enjoy celebrating Easter together. (Luke 24:33-35)

Lamb of God is a Living Savior. (John 1:29)

Matthew is a book that gives an account of the events. (Matthew 26-28)

Napkin was left behind when Jesus left the tomb. (John 20: 6-7 KJV)

Open tomb made a way for the women to enter. (Luke 24:1-3)

Peter was an eye-witness to the Risen Lord. (John 21)

Quotes from the cross included "It is finished." (John 19:30)

Resurrection of Christ leads to resurrection of believers.

(1 Corinthians 15:21-23)

Spices were included in the cloth wrappings of Christ's body.
(John 19:40)

Tomb Jesus was buried in was borrowed. (Matthew 27:57-60)

Upper room was used for Jesus and His disciples to eat the Passover meal. (Mark 14:15; Luke 22:12)

Victory over death and the grave was won. (1Corinthians 15:54)

Willingness of Christ to suffer and die for you and me was shown.
(Luke 22:42)

X, the Greek letter Xi(Chi), used in the symbol Chi Rho, ☧ , the first two letters in the Greek word Christos, meaning Christ.

Yielding to the Father's will, Christ died to bring us salvation.
(Matthew 26:39)

Zealous Peter cut off the soldier Malchus' ear, but Jesus, knowing His assignment, healed even one who came to arrest Him. (John 18:10; Luke 22:50-51)

"He is not here; for He is risen, as He said. Come, see the place where the Lord lay."(Matthew 28:6)

School Days from A to Z

Give instruction to a wise man, and he will be still wiser; Teach a just man, and he will increase in learning. (Proverbs 9:9)

Most children look forward to starting school. Now children begin preschool at two years old. When I began school, I was six, so eager to enter first grade. I enjoyed every grade, though seventh was rough. Many of my best friends had moved to a different building, plus I felt, probably without just cause, that my teacher did not like me. Fond memories of school days linger.

Alarms sound for students and faculty to practice drills for fire, weather, or safety.

Books are distributed and students quickly look inside the front cover to see who had that book in prior years.

Classrooms need to be found, and occasionally changed, and teachers need to be met.

Discipline bodes as necessary for learning, whether the correction is met with putting one's head on a desk, sitting behind a door, standing in the hall, writing a statement over and over, staying in during recess, or some kind of suspension.

Each student views his or her assignments, classmates, and teachers differently.

Friendships form that last a lifetime.

Gym is looked forward to by many, tolerated by others, and actually despised by a few. Learning different dances comes with this class.

Heroes emerge in the form of administrators, teachers, coaches, upperclassmen, or classmates.

In a few cases, students do not enjoy school, and do not go back to celebrations or reunions.

Jump rope is one of the most popular recess activities. Jumping double ropes or jumping double with a friend makes the endeavor even more fun. How about "Norma and Don sitting in a tree, K-I-S-S-I-N-G. How many kisses did he give her? One, two, three, four..."

Kisses are stolen at recess or in a vacant room after lunch.

Lunch ladies smile, greet warmly, and give big helpings.

Math is taught at every level, and is the favorite subject for some and the least favorite for others.

No other school quite compares to the one you attended.

Occasional bad grades on assignments spur students to try harder and realize the benefits of studying. If this happens too often or after intense study, bad grades bring discouragement.

Plays such as The Sound of Music, The Wizard of Oz, The Little Mermaid, and Beauty and the Beast give aspiring actors and actresses experience and excitement.

Quiet time during the day of kindergarten provides a needed break in the action.

Reading is such an essential in life. I went into first grade not being able to read a word and came out nine months later reading almost anything. I still am amazed that my first grade teacher could bring about that accomplishment.

Simply learning facts falls way short of the immense education offered during school days.

Teachers love and care for students in ways other than academics.

Understanding others, learning how people are different, and developing relationships is a huge part of school days.

Victory and defeat teach needed lessons to participants in athletic events, music contests, and academic contests.

Willing workers enjoy handing out graded papers, calling the roll, or rearranging desks.

eXercises come as a title for lots of work in textbooks. Students like it when the teacher says they can work the odd or even problems, or answer the odd or even questions, and not answer them all.

Year-end tests measure a student's progress in each subject for the year, but most learning does not come from books.

Zzzzzz come on Saturdays, holidays, and summer vacation. Students definitely look forward to those sleep-in times.

A disciple is not above his teacher, but everyone who is perfectly trained will be like his teacher. (Luke 6:40)

Songs of Praise and Worship from A to Z

"...but be filled with the Spirit, speaking to one another in psalms and hymns and spiritual songs, singing and making melody in your heart to the Lord, giving thanks always for all things to God the Father in the name of our Lord Jesus Christ," (Ephesians 5:18b-20)

Music speaks to the heart. Singing can be uplifting, comforting, soothing, exciting and so much more. Think of songs you enjoy as I share these.

Amazing Grace

Because He Lives

Come, Thou Fount of Every Blessing

Down at the Cross

Everybody Ought to Go to Sunday School

Forever

Glorious Day

Here I Am to Worship

I Bowed on My Knees and Cried Holy

Jesus Loves Me

Knowing You, Jesus

Lord, I Lift Your Name on High

Make Me a Blessing

Never Alone

Only Trust Him

Put Your Hand in the Hand

Quiet My Mind, Make Me Still Before You

Rejoice, the Lord is King

Shout to the Lord

The Old Rugged Cross

Up Calvary's Mountain (first line)

Victory in Jesus

When the Roll is Called up Yonder

e**X**odus, Theme from

You Are My All in All

O, **Z**ion Haste

"I will sing to the Lord as long as I live; I will sing praise to my God while I have my being." (Psalm 104:33)

Thoughts about Family from A to Z

"And these words which I command you today shall be in your heart. You shall teach them diligently to your children, and shall talk of them when you sit in your house, when you walk by the way, when you lie down, and when you rise up." (Deuteronomy 6:6-7)

Family comes in different shapes and sizes. When we talk about family, we can mean the family we grew up in, the family we live with now, or even our church family. I noticed many basketball teams from high schools to March Madness have Family emblazoned on their jerseys or warm-up shirts. I have some thoughts on Family from A to Z.

Always give bedtime hugs and kisses.
Backyards are wonderful places for playing, swinging, and learning to get along.
Closeness has nothing to do with distance.
Devotions together every day are glue for a family.
Eating together is essential.
Family is the foundation for our lives.
God is the Center of a successful family.
Helping each other is a priority.
Individuals are different, yet so much alike.
Just hanging out makes for a wonderful evening.
Keeping a journal to be read later stores lots of material for laughter.
Love is never a question.
Memories are precious.

Never go to bed mad. That's Scripture. (Ephesians 4:26)

Outsiders are not allowed to say anything negative about the family I love.

Pictures have to be taken regularly.

Quick to forgive needs to be standard procedure.

Riding in a car for a two-week vacation is an emotional challenge, but worth the effort.

Stories grow with time.

Together is my favorite place.

Understanding of others' wants and needs is necessary.

Vacations together are fun.

Working together makes chores easier.

Xylose is a type of sugar, but not as sweet as family.

Yesterday is gone, so love on them all you can today!

Zing go the strings of my heart in their presence.

"I'm so glad I'm a part of the family of God-..."
Words and Music by William J. Gaither © 1970 William J. Gaither, Inc.

Ways God Guides Us from A to Z

"I will instruct you and teach you in the way you should go; I will guide you with My eye." (Psalm 32:8)

God gives us guidelines and guardrails to keep us on the path and journey with Him. Many of these ways He guides us are found in Psalm 119. Others are throughout Scripture.

Advice for successful living is given by Solomon. "My son, do not forget my law, but let your heart keep my commands; for length of days and long life and peace they will add to you." (Proverbs 3:1-2)

Beatitudes given by Jesus in His Sermon on the Mount provide means for receiving blessings as each begins "Blessed are..." (Matthew 5:1-12)

Commandments cited throughout God's Word give us boundaries to live within. "Then I would not be ashamed, when I look into all Your commandments." (Psalm 119:6)

Direction awaits those who follow Jesus. "Trust in the Lord with all your heart, and lean not on your own understanding; in all your ways acknowledge Him, and He shall direct your paths." (Proverbs 3:5-6)

Establishment of His covenant assures us of His faithfulness to His promises. "...He is also Mediator of a better covenant, which was established on better promises." (Hebrews 8:6)

Faithfulness to Christ is rewarded, according to God's Word, with the servant's hearing, "Well done, good and faithful servant..." (Matthew 25:21)

Guidance can come from others who follow Christ. "Where there is no counsel, the people fall; but in the multitude of counselors there is safety. (Proverbs 11:14)

Holy Spirit conviction keeps us on the right path. "And when He has come, He will convict the world of sin, and of righteousness, and of judgment:" (John 16:8)

Instruction and teaching by God show us His way. "I will instruct you and teach you in the way you should go; I will guide you with My eye." (Psalm 32:8)

Judgments from God come to help us. "Let my soul live, and it shall praise You; and let Your judgments help me." (Psalm 119:175)

Knowledge for wise living comes from God and His Word. "Teach me good judgment and knowledge, for I believe Your commandments." (Psalm 119:66)

Laws are practiced and enforced to provide us abundant life. "Blessed are the undefiled in the way, who walk in the law of the Lord!" (Psalm 119:1)

Meditation on the laws of God gives us insight into their purpose. "Oh, how I love Your law! It is my meditation all the day." (Psalm 119:97)

Naming the laws one by one reinforces getting to know them. "But the mercy of the Lord is from everlasting to everlasting...to those who remember His commandments to do them." (Psalm 103:17-18)

Ordinances give hope to those who obey them. "And take not the word of truth utterly out of my mouth, for I have hoped in Your ordinances." (Psalm 119:43)

Precepts given by the Lord and obeyed bring life. "I will never forget Your precepts, for by them You have given me life." (Psalm 119:93)

Queues of directions to follow the teachings of Christ can be found in the chapters of God's Word. (Matthew 5-7)

Righteousness from God through faith in Christ leads us through life. "Lead me, O Lord, in Your righteousness because of my enemies; make Your way straight before my face. (Psalm 5:8)

Statutes direct our ways to follow Christ. "Oh, that my ways were directed to keep Your statutes!" (Psalm 119:5)

Truth from God sets us free. "And you shall know the truth, and the truth shall make you free." (John 8:32)

Understanding comes from knowing God's goodness so we can avoid wrongdoing. "Through Your precepts I get understanding; therefore I hate every false way." (Psalm 119:104)

Visions from God to the prophets of the Old Testament give insight into the glory of and ways of God. (Ezekiel 8; Daniel 2; Joel 2; Amos 7-8; Obadiah 1; Nahum 1)

Word of God guides us in following Him. "Your Word is a lamp to my feet and a light to my path." (Psalm 119:105)

eXpectation of God's fulfillment of His promises helps us keep on keeping on. "My soul, wait silently for God alone, for my expectation is from Him." (Psalm 62:5)

Your Name is powerful and helpful in many situations. "Therefore God also has highly exalted Him and given Him the name which is above every name, that at the name of Jesus every knee should bow,..." (Philippians 2:9-10)

Zero times we will not be forgiven if we fail in following His guidance. "If we confess our sins, He is faithful and just to forgive us our sins and to cleanse us from all unrighteousness." (1 John 1:9)

"All Scripture is given by inspiration of God, and is profitable for doctrine, for reproof, for correction, for instruction in righteousness,"
(2 Timothy 3:16)

What Jesus Came to Do from A to Z

"For I have come down from heaven, not to do My own will, but the will of Him who sent Me." (John 6:38)

Jesus came to:

Atone for sins. (Hebrews 7:26-27)

Bind up the broken. (Isaiah 61:1)

Call disciples to follow Him. (Matthew 4:19)

Die. (Mark 10:45)

Engage others. (Matthew 22:17-21)

Forgive. (Luke 5:20)

Give "Living Water." (John 7:38)

Heal. (Matthew 4:23)

Invite others to "Come unto Me." (Matthew 11:28)

Judge. (2 Timothy 4:1)

Know the hearts of people. (Luke 9:47)

Love. (Mark 10:21)

Make "all things new." (2 Corinthians 5:17)

Nudge others to love each other. (John 15:12)

Open blind eyes and hearts. (Matthew 20:32-34)

Pray and **P**reach. (Mark 1:35-39)

Quiet restless souls. (Luke 8:26-35)

Raise the dead. (John 11:43-44)

Seek and **S**ave. (Luke 19:10)

Touch (Luke 5:12-13) and Teach. (Mark 4:1)

Unseat Satan from the throne on men's hearts. (Luke 22:31)

Verify prophecies of the Old Testament. (Matthew 27:35; 21:4-5; 13:14)

Write a new chapter in the history of the world. (Luke 23:44-46; 24:6)

X-ray souls to know motives and thoughts. (Luke 5:22)

Yield to the will of the Father. (Matthew 26:39)

Zero in on each individual. (John 3:3)

"I have come that they may have life, and that they may have it more abundantly." (John 10:10)

What to Do on Rainy Days from A to Z

"The LORD will open to you His good treasure, the heavens, to give the rain to your land in its season, and to bless all the work of your hand."
(Deuteronomy 28:12)

On a rainy day…

Arrange your furniture differently.

Be lazy.

Clean out a closet.

Dance to a favorite song.

Exercise with a video.

Forget the errands you planned to run.

Go back to bed.

Have an extra cup of coffee or tea.

Initiate a meal delivery chain for a sick friend.

Just hang around in your pajamas.

Knit.

Listen to the rhythm of the falling rain.

Make cookies or candy.

Neatly fold fitted sheets.

Organize a junk drawer.

Play solitaire.

Quietly pray for each of your Facebook friends, and those who are not on social media.

Relax and read a good book.

Sleep late and snuggle with family or your pet.

Telephone a friend or family member you haven't talked to in awhile.

Undo a knot in a jewelry chain or shoe string.

Vacuum under your bed.

Write on the back of pictures.

e**X**tend your Bible reading and studying time.

Yawn, yawn, and yawn some more.

Zigzag from activity to activity at your pleasure.

*"For the earth which drinks in the rain that often comes upon it,
and bears herbs useful for those by whom it is cultivated,
receives blessing from God;" (Hebrews 6:7)*

When A Trumpet Sounds from A to Z

"With trumpets and the sound of a horn; Shout joyfully before the Lord, the King." (Psalm 98:6)

We enjoy the sound of a trumpet for our musical entertainment. Without the means of communication we have today, trumpets are used throughout the Bible for myriad and serious purposes.

At the sound of the trumpet...

Alarm is signaled. (Numbers 10:9)

Be on alert. (Exodus 19:16)

Come for an announcement. (Exodus 19:13)

Dead in Christ will rise. (1 Corinthians 15:52)

Equipping for a job is at hand. (Judges 7:16)

Follow the leader. (Joshua 6:8)

Gather. (Numbers 10:4; Jeremiah 4:5)

Holy convocation may begin. (Numbers 29:1)

Incorruption will follow for believers. (1 Corinthians 15:52)

Joyful noise will break forth. (Psalm 98:6)

King Jesus will appear. (1 Thessalonians 4:16)

Listen to what is being said. (Isaiah 18:3; Exodus 19:19)

Memorials are offered. (Leviticus 25:9; Numbers 10:10)

No service work is to be done when holy convocation is announced. (Numbers 29:1)

Ordinance may be established forever. (Numbers 10:8)

Praise may begin. (Psalm 150:3)

Quick response is required. (Judges 7:17-22)

Resurrection could be happening. (1 Corinthians 15:52)

Shouting may be called for. (Joshua 6:5)

Travel is to begin. Get ready to go. (Numbers 10:2; Judges 3:27)

Utter chaos should turn to order as a message is heard.
(1 Corinthians 14:8)

Victory is sounded as a mission is accomplished. (Joshua 6:20)

War may be imminent. (Numbers 10:9; 31:6)

eXtended warning of attack may be given. (Ezekiel 33:1-6)

You may be at a funeral where taps is played to honor a soldier.
(Job 30:31)

Zeal may be called for to assemble and cry out. (Jeremiah 4:5)

*"in a moment, in the twinkling of an eye, at the last trumpet. For the
trumpet will sound, and the dead will be raised incorruptible,
and we shall be changed." (1 Corinthians 15:52)*

*"For the Lord Himself will descend from heaven with a shout, with the
voice of an archangel, and with the trumpet of God.
And the dead in Christ will rise first." (1 Thessalonians 4:16)*

Words I Think of When I Consider Heaven
from A to Z

"Nevertheless we, according to His promise, look for new heavens and a new earth in which righteousness dwells." (2 Peter 3:13)

Angels—created beings who live in Heaven (Galatians 1:8; Colossians 1:16)

Beautiful—a place of glory and honor (Revelation 21:23-24)

Crystal Sea—flows from the throne of God (Revelation 4:6)

Described in Revelation—(Revelation 21)

Elders—twenty-four who worship at the throne and cast their crowns before Him who sits on the throne (Revelation 4:10)

Friends—People will be gathered from all the earth for all of Heaven. (Mark 13:27; Revelation 5:9)

Gates of Pearl—Each of twelve gates is one pearl. (Revelation 21:21)

High—above all things, above the earth and firmament (Psalm 103:11; Ezekiel 1:26)

Imagine—The Bible says we cannot see or hear all that is prepared for us. (1 Corinthians 2:9)

Jesus—will be there! (John 14:1-4)

Know all things—as He knows us now (1 Corinthians 13:12)

Light never ceases—The Lamb is the Light (Revelation 21:23)

Martyrs—Those killed for their faith in Christ (Revelation 6:9)

No more night—city always open (Revelation 21:25)

Open arms of Jesus—He receives us. (John 14:3)

Promised—to those who trust Jesus as Savior (John 3:16; 2 Peter 3:13)

Quickened souls—will rise (1 Thessalonians 4:16)

River—clear as crystal (Revelation 22:1-2)

Streets of Gold—we will walk on (Revelation 21:21b)

Tears are gone—no more crying or sorrow (Revelation 21:4)

Understanding—we will know the "whys" (1 Corinthians 13:12)

Viewed now with limited sight (1 Corinthians 13:12)

Windows—that open (Genesis 7:11; 2 Kings 7:2; Malachi 3:10)

eXtreme—more than we can think of or imagine (1 Corinthians 2:9)

Yummy—There will be a banquet. (Revelation 19:9)

Zenith—Heaven is the highest place we can gain for every aspect of our lives. (Revelation 3:12)

"In My Father's house are many mansions; if it were not so, I would have told you. I go to prepare a place for you. And if I go and prepare a place for you, I will come again and receive you to Myself; that where I am, there you may be also." (John 14:2-3)

Worship Is... from A to Z

*"God is Spirit, and those who worship Him must worship
in spirit and truth." (John 4:24)*

Worship is...

Adoration of the Heavenly Father.

Bowing before the Almighty God.

Confessing sin.

Deciding to let God change our lives.

Entering into our closets to pray.

Finding God in everything around us.

Giving ourselves to studying God's Word.

Having faith in difficult situations.

Inviting God to direct our paths.

Journeying daily with the Master of the universe.

Knowing we are guided by the Holy Spirit.

Learning obedience to our heavenly Father.

Making time for Bible study and prayer.

Naming the Name above all names.

Opening our hearts to hear from the Father.

Praying to and praising the Father.

Quietly listening for His still, small voice.

Remembering what Christ did for us.

Singing praise to the Father, Son, and Holy Spirit.

Tithing to our local body of Christ and giving an offering.

Uniting our spirits with the Spirit of God.

Visiting God through His Word.

Wanting to honor the King of Kings and Lord of Lords.

e**X**amining our lives in light of God's Word.

Yielding our wills to the will of God.

Zeroing in on the one and only Son of God.

*"Give to the Lord the glory due His name; Bring an offering, and come
before Him. Oh, worship the Lord in the beauty of holiness!"*
(1 Chronicles 16:29)

EPILOGUE

In March of 2017 my sweet daughter-in-law Heather gave me the opportunity to speak in chapel to the Lower School students of Providence Christian Academy in Murfreesboro, Tennessee. Their theme for that quarter was Onward: Stretch and Grow. Wanting to give them words of wisdom from a grandmother, yet something fun so they would want to listen, I asked them to participate by going through their ABC's for the guidance I proposed for each letter. The following pages in *Loving Life from A to Z* contain the transcript of that program.

ONWARD: STRETCH AND GROW
from A to Z

      Good morning PCA Lower School! You sound ready to move onward, to stretch and grow. Mr. McMurry and I have wonderful grandchildren at PCA who keep growing in more ways than one. They are about to grow up on us. Many of you know Trey, Grace, Zach and Max. I am so honored to be with you today.

      One of the first things you learn, even in preparation to come to preschool, is your ABC's. Remember when you were a tiny kid how fun it was to sing your alphabet? Today we are going to see how we can stretch and grow through using the alphabet. Onward: Stretch and Grow from A to Z.

Allow God's Word to be your Guide.

"Thy Word is a Lamp unto my feet and a Light unto my path."(Psalm 119:105 KJV) His Word will lead you onward, and many times you will have to stretch and grow to obey what God has in store for you. Proverbs 3:5-6 tells us "Trust in the Lord with all your heart, And lean not on your own understanding; In all your ways acknowledge Him, And He shall direct your paths."

Believe God's Promises.

Sometimes you can get discouraged. In our world lots of things happen that we do not understand. You begin to doubt, doubt even that God really loves you. God has given us "great and precious promises," (2 Peter 1:4) and in Christ Jesus "all the promises of God in Him are Yes, and in Him Amen," (2 Corinthians 1:20)

Count your blessings.

There is an old hymn whose words are "name them one by one." Be sure to include blessings you take for granted and are around every day—like your family, your pet, food, and even when your mom or dad says, "No," because they love you.

Dare to do activities and events that are new to you.

Get involved in service projects. Run for office. Play a sport. Try out for the play. You might not do as well at everything as some other students do, but that's okay. You'll never know how you are at something or if you like it unless you try it. And if you don't enjoy it, do something else next time.

Energize others around you to be their best.

Encourage your friends and classmates. Compliment them when they do something well. Sometimes we think, "Oh, she's so good at that," but we never tell the person. Tell them.

Find a new way to do something you need to do but don't enjoy. Study in a different place. Sing while you do a chore for your parents. When Mr. McMurry was a little boy, he would sing to the top of his lungs while he pulled the trash can to the road. When you accomplish your hard task, perhaps your parents will let you have a treat.

Get up off the couch and do something new and fun and helpful. Write a poem for your mom. Pick some flowers, not without permission, from your neighbor's yard, and put them in a vase on the dinner table. Make place cards for your family at dinner, or make a card for a sick friend.

Help someone with a task they need to do, even your brother or sister. Surprise them by offering to help with the dishes when it is not your turn. Go to the other side of the bed and offer to help make it. If you are the older sibling, offer to help with homework or read to a little brother or sister.

Invite someone different to be with you or you and your already friends when you do an activity. There are new students at school, and maybe even to Murfreesboro. Invite a new person to church with you.

Jump! That means be active. Everyone needs some kind of exercise every day. You have gym and recess at school. Be sure you take part and have fun enjoying your classmates. Other activities can include riding a bike, skating, or swimming. Stay active.

Keep your heart.

Proverbs 4:23 tells us to "Keep your heart with all diligence, For out of it spring the issues of life." When you keep something you take care of it and guard it. That is what we need to do with the thoughts we have and the actions we take. Let love and goodness spring from you, and keep out bad thoughts like jealousy and dislike.

Learn all you can this year from your teachers, classmates, and parents. They really know a lot and want to help you learn. You can learn your class material, and you can learn a lot more. Listening to how others talk can teach you what to say in situations. Watching the actions of others can be lessons for you to see how to act in various circumstances.

Make this year your best school year ever! Know that good things are coming your way. Participate in every activity when you are able. The more you put into anything, the more you gain from it. Invest your time and your energy in what is provided here at school to be your best self.

Nail down your faith, knowing that Jesus is "the Way, the Truth, and the Life." Faith is personal. You are not a Christian because your mother and daddy believe in Christ or your grandmother and granddaddy believe. Your faith is your own! No one else's. Jesus died for you.

Open your eyes and ears to what is around you. Don't miss something good. When your parents ask you, "What went on at school today?," don't ever be able to say, "Nothing." Give an answer even if is, "My friend fell out of the swing," or "Lunch surely was good," or our headmaster Dr. Mott rode a bicycle down the hall giving everyone ice cream." You'll learn a lot by paying attention to your surroundings.

Put on the whole armor of God every day. Paul tells us in Ephesians 6 to take our stands for Christ. And then he tells us to put on armor to protect ourselves from evil around us. Have truth around your waist as your belt. Belts hold everything together and in place. Put on righteousness to protect your heart and vital organs. A soldier's boots in Bible times were of bronze or heavy metal. They wore them so they were prepared to march on thorns and sticks that would normally hurt their feet. They were prepared to walk so they could have peace. We can have peace with God, peace with ourselves, and peace with others. The shield is faith so you can stand for Jesus no matter what comes your way. The helmet of salvation protects your mind and your thoughts. With your armor on, you then use your sword of the Spirit, which is the word of God. God's word will show you the way for all your lives. Paul then tells us to pray always.

Question what people tell you—in a good way.

In Acts 17:11 the people of Berea listened to Paul, then they studied what he said. They looked at Scripture to make sure it was true. It's like if someone tells you God didn't create the world. Check it out with Scripture and be able to say, "Yes He did! The Bible says so."

Read as much as you can.

You can travel the world. You can meet kings and queens and inventors and cowboys and sportspeople and anyone you want to. You can learn about men and women of long ago, or of today. Read as much as you can.

Sing lots and loud!

Music can be felt whether you know the notes or not. There are lots and lots of plaques about music and life. "Music says things words can't say." "Music always helps." When our children grew up and moved away, I told my husband, "What I miss the most is the music." Our kids were always singing or whistling.

Take time to have fun.

Laugh and be able to laugh at yourself. Laughter is good medicine. Proverbs 17:22 tells us "A merry heart does good like a medicine." And don't take yourself too seriously. If you do something that makes others want to laugh, laugh with them.

Use that with which God has blessed you.

Each of you has abilities and talents unique to you. God made you special. If you can sing, sing. If you can run fast, run fast. If you understand math and science, study it. Psalm 139:14 tells us that each of us is "fearfully and wonderfully made." Go with how you are made.

Venture into the unknown.

Who here is at PCA for the first time? You have ventured into a world that was unknown to you until July. For each of you, maybe there is something you have been wanting to know about. Find out about it.

Write in a journal or diary or blog.

When you are older you will enjoy looking back at your daily life. We think we can remember what goes on in our worlds, but we can't. You'll really be glad if you will do this. Even if you don't write every day, record much of what you do or think.

X-out negative things that come your

way. If you make a grade you are not happy with, don't fret too long. Tell yourself you will use that to study differently, or study more, or ask for help for the next test. X-out unkind words or actions from your life. You know the Golden Rule. "Do unto others as you would have them do unto you." The Bible says it "Therefore, whatever you want men to do to you, do also to them, for this is the Law and the Prophets." (Matthew 7:12) My mother used to tell me often, "No man goes his way alone. What you wish into the lives of others, comes back into your own."

Yell at pep rallies with all your

might! That's when you are supposed to be loud! And at games the Lions play, you can be Biblical when you shout, hopefully with "the voice of triumph." (Psalm 47:1)

Zip your mouth when you are

supposed to, like when your teacher is talking, and Zoom to new heights in all you do. Your parents and teachers are wonderful guides. They want you to do your very best; they want you to succeed in all you do, and thrive in areas of your special gifts. Head onward, stretching and growing each day.

And now, let's sing together the ABC song. Sing A-Z normally, then sing "won't you stretch and grow with me?"

ABOUT THE AUTHOR

Norma Williams McMurry grew up in eastern North Carolina, in the small town of Robersonville. Her interests in First Baptist Church, endeavors in the Robersonville Schools, occupation at Williams Red and White grocery store, and activities of family and friends encouraged Norma to take pleasure in and benefit from every aspect of life.

Wake Forest College provided four years of Camelot for Norma. She earned a Bachelor of Science in chemistry and found her football-playing preacher husband, Don McMurry. While Don attended school, Norma taught chemistry and math, and earned a Certificate from The Evening School of The Southern Baptist Theological Seminary in Louisville, Kentucky.

The McMurrys pastored and taught school thirty-seven years in Ohio and six years in Missouri. During that time, Norma earned a Master of Arts in counseling from Liberty University. Now married fifty-four years, the McMurrys reside in Fayetteville, Georgia. Don continues to help churches as interim pastor. They enjoy their three grown children their spouses, and ten grandchildren.

Norma incorporated Giving Thanks Ministries, through which she speaks and writes with the goal of encouraging joyous and purposeful living through Jesus Christ.